MORRISEY ON PLANNING

A Guide to Long-Range Planning

MORRISEY ON PLANNING

A Guide to Long-Range Planning

Creating Your Strategic Journey

George L. Morrisey

Jossey-Bass Publishers • San Francisco

Substantial discounts on bulk quantities of Jossey-Bass books are
available to corporations, professional associations, and other
organizations. For details and discount information, contact the
special sales department at Jossey-Bass Inc., Publishers.
(415) 433-1740; Fax (800) 605-2665.

For sales outside the United States, please contact your local
Simon & Schuster International Office.

Manufactured in the United States of America.

Library of Congress Cataloging-in-Publication Data

Morrisey, George L.
    Morrisey on planning : a guide to long-range planning : creating your
strategic journey / George L. Morrisey.
       p.   cm. — (Jossey-Bass business and management series)
    Includes bibliographical references and index.
    ISBN 0-7879-0169-5
    1. Strategic planning. I. Title. II. Series.
HD30.28.M653   1996
658.4'012—dc20   95-23793
                                                CIP

FIRST EDITION
HB Printing   10 9 8 7 6 5 4 3 2 1

THE JOSSEY-BASS BUSINESS AND MANAGEMENT SERIES

THE
MORRISEY ON PLANNING
SERIES

A Guide to Strategic Thinking
Building Your Planning Foundation

A Guide to Long-Range Planning
Creating Your Strategic Journey

A Guide to Tactical Planning
Producing Your Short-Term Results

Contents

What Should Be Your Future Positions? Determining Your Long-Term Objectives   51

How Will You Reach Your Future Positions? Preparing Your Strategic Action Plans   63

CHAPTER SEVEN
How Will You Know Where You Are?
Reviewing and Modifying Your Strategic Plan

CHAPTER EIGHT
How Does Your Strategic Plan Come Together?

Introduction to the Series

My experience in working with the planning process over a period of many years with a wide variety of client organizations has led me to the conclusion that there are three phases managers must go through in this process, each characterized by a distinctly different mind-set. The first phase is *strategic thinking*, which focuses on the more *intuitive* aspects of the process leading to the development of the organization's mission, vision, and strategy. This phase is designed to create the organization's future *perspective* while establishing a foundation from which all major planning decisions will be made.

The second phase is *long-range planning*, which calls for a combination of intuitive and *analytical* thinking leading to projections of future *positions* the organization wishes to attain. This phase is designed to validate and activate the mission, vision, and strategy created during the first phase.

The third phase is *tactical planning*, which is primarily an analytical approach with some intuitive overtones that leads to specific actions affecting the organization's current *performance*. This phase is designed to produce the short-term results needed to carry out the organization's mission and to reach the future positions that have been projected.

I have established this three-book series to reflect how several of my clients have chosen to work through the planning process. By design, the books are

- Short, practical, and how-to oriented. They are a length that is more comfortable for most managers than many of the longer, more theoretical books on the subject.

- Easily portable and appropriate for introspective reading during quiet times (such as on an airplane trip).

- Designed as an interrelated series, yet each book stands on its own as a guide to doing a more effective job on the aspect of planning addressed in that particular book.

- Useful source materials for seminars and workshops on planning; they also may be used as pre-reading and advance assignments for facilitated planning events and as ongoing reference books for individual managers and management teams as they work with the process on the job.

The first book, *A Guide to Strategic Thinking: Building Your Planning Foundation*, will help you get your planning team started by determining your organization's principles and values as well as the strategic direction in which you should be moving. While there is heavier emphasis in this book on the roles of the CEO and the senior management team, it provides guidance for all managers throughout your organization who must contribute to the strategic planning process.

The second book, *A Guide to Long-Range Planning: Creating Your Strategic Journey*, provides the tools for establishing a focus on the positions toward which your organization needs to strive in such areas as future markets, future products and services, technology, human competencies, and financial projections. It will be useful for all managers in your organization who need to focus on the future.

The third book, *A Guide to Tactical Planning: Producing Your Short-Term Results*, will provide all managers (executives, middle managers, first-line supervisors, and individual contributors alike) with a methodology for achieving meaningful short-term results on both a planned and an ad hoc basis.

The brief nature of each book makes this series a resource that participating managers can easily use on an ongoing basis as well as in preparing for formal planning efforts. While the emphasis in each use will be different, all managers have a vested interest in making both the strategic and tactical planning processes work in their areas of responsibility. All of the books contain examples drawn from individual departments and work units as well as from the perspective of the total organization. Some of these examples are identified as coming from specific organizations with which I have worked. Others represent adaptations from the efforts of organizations I have chosen not to identify. All of the examples are real.

As with any set of tools, the effective use of these books is dependent upon the desire and skill of the person using them. They are not designed as a substitute for sound managerial judgment. Rather, they are intended to enhance that judgment in order to help you and other managers in your organization do a more consistent and creative job of planning to meet future as well as current needs. Best wishes in your journey!

Acknowledgments

I have been privileged to be associated with many of the top management thinkers of our time. They have significantly influenced my work, as resources and in many cases as direct collaborators. They include, of course, my two previous coauthors of Jossey-Bass publications—*The Executive Guide to Strategic Planning* and *The Executive Guide to Operational Planning*—Patrick Below and Betty Acomb, as well as Bonnie Abney, Louis Allen, N. H. Atthreya, Joe Batten, Arthur Beck, Fred Clark, Donn Coffee, Tom Connellan, Peter Drucker, Marie Kane, Alec Mackenzie, Bob Mager, Dale McConkey, Henry Migliore, Howard Mold, George Odiorne, Gene Seyna, Brian Tracy, and Glenn Varney.

I am especially appreciative of the many fine managers within the organizations I have served as a consultant, who have allowed me the opportunity to validate the concepts and techniques of effective planning while providing me with excellent feedback that helped immeasurably in refinement of the process. I would like particularly to acknowledge two outstanding managers who have demonstrated how this process can work effectively over a long period of time in a variety of increasingly responsible positions: Chris Ellefson of BHP Minerals International and Nelson Marchioli of Burger King.

I have been blessed to be associated for several years with a group of professional speakers, trainers, and consultants that we, its members, refer to as our mentor group. These colleagues have encouraged, critiqued, and otherwise helped me to hone my ideas and to properly position my publications as well as my services to clients. They are Tom Callister, Lola Gillebaard, Jane Holcomb, Eileen McDargh, Jack Mixner, and Karen Wilson.

Finally, but far from least, I will be eternally grateful for the continuous support I receive from my business partner, my best friend, and my loving wife for many years, Carol Morrisey.

Merritt Island, Florida   G.L.M.
April 1995

Preface

Portions of the present book were adapted from a book I coauthored with Patrick J. Below and Betty L. Acomb in 1987 entitled *The Executive Guide to Strategic Planning*. That book explored both *strategic thinking* and *long-range planning*. However, as indicated in the introduction to this series, my experience since that time in assisting many client organizations with the planning process has prompted me to address strategic thinking and long-range planning in two separate books because of the distinct differences in both developing and implementing these two planning processes. I have also made several modifications in the long-range planning process as first introduced in the earlier book. The present book reflects the way I am currently assisting clients in making long-range planning work for them.

The first substantive change is the introduction of the planning element *Key Strategic Areas* (KSAs). This is a variation on *Key Results Areas* (KRAs), which has been an element in the tactical or operational planning process for many years. KSAs represent those major categories on which collective attention must be focused for the foreseeable future. They are broader in scope than KRAs and are designed to help you determine where you want to be as an organization rather than the specific results you want to achieve.

A number of my clients have found it useful for two reasons to identify their KSAs *before* going through the *critical issue analysis* process. First, some *Long-Term Objectives* (LTOs) can be determined directly from KSAs without going through an in-depth analysis, because they are predetermined by a parent organization's plan or other high-level plan, because they are a carryover from a previous plan, or because they are obvious, based on the organization's established strategy. The second reason is that KSAs are a helpful vehicle for identifying and categorizing critical issues that need to be analyzed.

Critical issue analysis is a derivation of *strategic analysis*, which was an element of *strategic thinking*, discussed in *The Executive Guide to Strategic Planning*. Because of the analytical nature of strategic analysis, I have found it to be useful as an early step in the long-range planning process, after mission, vision, and strategy have been determined. I have also made more extensive use of the SLOTs Assessment (Strengths, Limitations, Opportunities, and Threats), as well as of critical issue analysis as an ongoing process for addressing strategic concerns.

Strategic Action Plans (SAPs) are a variation on what was called *integrated programs* in the earlier book. The emphasis in strategic action plans is on identifying major events, phases, or accomplishments to be completed on the road to attaining future positions identified as long-term objectives. I have also introduced the use of *decision trees* as a means for preparing plans that may change significantly over time based on information that was not available or used at the outset.

Finally, I have added a chapter on *reviewing and modifying your strategic plan*, a process designed to close the loop on both strategic thinking and long-range planning.

How Can This Book Be Used?

I believe that the long-range planning process described in this book will be useful to managers at all levels who are responsible for charting the future of their organizations. There are several ways you can use this book, including as a:

- Guide for management teams preparing their long-range plans at both the total organization and unit levels.

- Guide for individual managers and management teams in their ongoing long-range planning efforts.

- Text for an in-house workshop on long-range planning skills for managers. The book is laid out in a logical manner that lends itself to a segmented instructional plan.

- Text for a college or university extension program or a public seminar on strategic planning. (Note: the content and examples are directed primarily toward participants who wish to apply them in their own work areas, not toward those studying management theory.)

- Reference guide for internal and external consultants charged with helping organizations and managers with their planning efforts.

- Individual study guide for the working manager.

For self-study, I recommend the following approach:

1.   Read the Preface and Chapters One, Two, and Eight for an overview of the planning philosophy and process being presented.

2.   Determine which of the following alternatives best serves your individual needs:

a. Selective learning of specific techniques to supplement your existing knowledge

b. Concentrating on learning the long-term objectives and strategic action planning steps for use in your individual or unit efforts

c. Concentrating on learning the critical issue analysis process as an ongoing process for addressing opportunities, threats, strengths, and limitations

d. Learning and applying the entire process to your job

3.   If you have selected 2(a) as most appropriate, the recommendation is easy. Study and practice those steps that will satisfy your needs.

4. If 2(b) seems best for you at the moment, Chapters Five and Six will be of most value. I recommend that you identify one important future position you would like to attain. Then, following the guidelines given, write out the long-term objective(s) and strategic action plan(s) required to make the position a reality. Concentrating on only one major effort will give you an opportunity to learn from the experience, after which the application of the entire long-range planning process can be further expanded as desired.

5. If 2(c) looks intriguing, go through Chapter Four. Then, take a particularly interesting opportunity and work through the analysis process with your team or as an individual. Resist the temptation to jump too quickly to the "solution" as the process may open some alternatives you had not previously considered. Also, you may discover that you are analyzing the wrong issue and a better clarification may occur.

6. If you are ready to commit yourself to 2(d), I recommend defining your key strategic areas first in order to segment areas on which your long-range planning efforts need to be focused. I then recommend proceeding selectively through the rest of the process in a few key areas, gradually working the approach into your entire operation.

7. Use the book as a continual reference, particularly Chapters Four and Eight and the various working tools and checklists, as you continue your application of the long-range planning process.

8. Don't get discouraged when you hit the inevitable periods of setback and frustration in application of this approach to long-range planning. Stay with it, and both your satisfaction and effectiveness will increase as you continue to develop your skill.

Get ready now to become an even more effective manager than you already are through the use of this practical, proven approach to long-range planning!

Merritt Island, Florida   G.L.M.
August 1995

The Author

George L. Morrisey is chairman of The Morrisey Group, a management consulting firm based in Merritt Island, Florida. He received his B.S. (1951) and M.Ed. (1952) from Springfield College. He has more than twenty years of experience as a practicing manager and key specialist with such organizations as the YMCA, First Western Bank, Rockwell International, McDonnell Douglas, and the U.S. Postal Service, as well as more than twenty years as a full-time consultant, professional speaker, and seminar leader. He has personally assisted more than two hundred business, industrial, service, governmental, and not-for-profit organizations throughout the world in the areas of strategic and tactical planning.

Morrisey is the author or coauthor of fifteen books prior to this series, including *Management by Objectives and Results in the Public Sector* (1976); *Management by Objectives and Results for Business and Industry* (1977); *Getting Your Act Together: Goal Setting for Fun, Health and Profit* (1980); *Performance Appraisals for Business and Industry* (1983); *Performance Appraisals in the Public Sector* (1983); *The Executive Guide to Operational Planning* (with Patrick J. Below and Betty L. Acomb, 1987); *The Executive Guide to Strategic Planning* (with Patrick J. Below and Betty L. Acomb, 1987); *Effective Business and Technical Presentations* (with Thomas L. Sechrest, 1987); and *Creating Your Future: Personal Strategic Planning for Professionals* (1992). He is the author and producer of several learning programs on audiocassette and videocassette, all directed toward helping individuals and organizations become more effective and self-fulfilled.

A professional's professional, Morrisey received the Certified Speaking Professional (CSP) designation in 1983 and was recognized in 1984 with the CPAE (Council of Peers Award for Excellence), the highest recognition granted to a professional speaker by the National Speakers Association. In addition, in 1994, Morrisey was the sixteenth annual recipient of the Cavett Award, named in honor of the founder of the National Speakers Association, Cavett Robert. Morrisey is a former member of the boards of directors of the Association for Management Excellence (originally the International MBO Institute) and the National Speakers Association.

For further information on Morrisey's services, please contact:

The Morrisey Group
P.O. Box 541296
Merritt Island, FL 32954-1296
(800) 535-8202, (407) 452-7414, Fax (407) 452-2129

A Guide to Long-Range Planning

CHAPTER ONE

How Do You Make the Future a Reality?

The Rest of the Strategic Planning Story

For many years, "strategic planning" and "long-range planning" were treated as synonyms. Unfortunately, long-range planning as it has been practiced in many organizations amounts to little more than an extrapolation of history. Managers review their results of the previous four or five years and project a similar pattern over the next four or five years, making adjustments for changes they know are going to take place. In today's ever-changing environment, such a practice represents a chartered trip to organizational oblivion. As one wag put it, *the only constant we can look forward to is change.* Some changes are inevitable while others will come as a result of our own creative efforts. An effective planning process must proactively address both.

The premise initiated in the first book in this series, *A Guide to Strategic Thinking*, can be reiterated here: that the planning process operates on a continuum between intuitive and analytical thought, as shown in Figure 1.1. It was this premise that led me to treat the planning process in three books, each based on one component of the process and where it falls on the continuum. The first component, *strategic thinking*, relies heavily on intuition, with only a modest amount of analysis. *Long-range planning* represents a balance between the two processes. *Tactical planning* is primarily based on analysis, with intuition serving largely as a check and balance.

In the first book I also introduced "the three P's" of the planning process: perspective, position, and performance. Each of the three major components of the planning process relates to the three P's as follows:

Intuitive ——————————————————————————— **Analytical**
Strategic Thinking   Long-Range Planning   Tactical Planning

Figure 1.1 The Planning Process Continuum

Strategic thinking leads to *perspective*

Long-range planning leads to *position*

Tactical planning leads to *performance*

While the three components naturally overlap, each of them requires a different level of thinking on the part of managers participating in the process. The components and their specific elements are shown in Figure 1.2. Note that each of the first two components penetrates the next one, leading the process from planning into effective implementation.

In this book, I stress the importance of looking at the horizon—where your organization needs to be at specific times in the future if you are to carry out the mission, vision, and strategy identified during the strategic thinking phase of your planning process.

What Is Long-Range Planning and Why Is It Important?

Long-range planning involves the application of both intuition and analysis to determining future *positions* your organization needs to attain. It also must be seen as a dynamic process that is flexible enough to allow and even encourage modification of plans in order to respond to changing circumstances. Long-range planning is important because

- It keeps you focused on the future as well as the present.
- It reinforces the principles espoused in your mission, vision, and strategy.
- It encourages cross-functional planning and communication.
- It prioritizes where resources are to be directed.

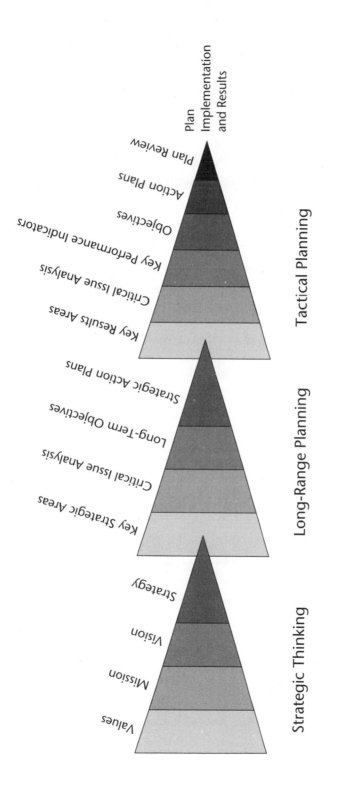

Figure 1.2 The Planning Process

Strategic Thinking

Values
Mission
Vision
Strategy

Long-Range Planning

Key Strategic Areas
Critical Issue Analysis
Long-Term Objectives
Strategic Action Plans

Tactical Planning

Key Results Areas
Critical Issue Analysis
Key Performance Indicators
Objectives
Action Plans
Plan Review

Plan Implementation and Results

- It builds a bridge to your short-term tactical planning process.
- It encourages managers to look at planning from a macro perspective, alerting them to core objectives so they can contribute to achieving them.

Long-range planning is a process that brings your management team together to translate your mission, vision, and strategy into tangible future results. It also saves valuable managerial time, reduces conflict, and encourages ownership and commitment to the efforts required to make your desired future a reality.

What's Involved in the Long-Range Planning Process?

Long-range planning is more of an analytical process than strategic thinking, although it still depends heavily on the intuitive knowledge, understanding, and judgment of participating managers. Regardless of the sophistication of the analytical tools used in the process, sound managerial judgment is still the cornerstone of effective long-range planning. Decisions must be made based on the collective judgment of those charged with the responsibility for your organization's future. This is why it is vital that your management team members agree on the nature and scope of your business, the principles under which you intend to operate, and the direction in which you should be moving as an organization—in other words, the results of your strategic thinking—*before* identifying specific destinations and routes of travel.

Here are brief descriptions of the four major elements that make up this approach to long-range planning:

- *Key Strategic Areas* (KSAs). These are the major categories on which collective attention must be focused for the foreseeable future. Many of the KSAs will be similar to the *Key Results Areas* (KRAs) that will be identified in tactical planning. However, the focus of KSAs is broader in scope and designed to help you determine where you want to be as an organization rather than the specific results you want to achieve. For example, the focus of *financial projections* as a KSA is more likely to be on such things as growth rates, net worth, and revenue mix, while the emphasis of *financial results*, as a KRA, is likely to be on specific product line revenues, gross/net profit, and cash flow. The focus of *product development* as a KSA would be to look more at new, long-lead-time products or services with significant future potential (in line with your mission and strategy), while viewing this area as a KRA would likely put the focus more on product modifications and new product releases that would contribute to your current year's bottom line.

The primary purpose in determining your KSAs first in the long-range planning process is to help you identify critical strategic issues that need to be addressed over an extended period of time if you are to carry out your mission and strategy. Having agreed on your KSAs as a management team will make the process of identifying and analyzing these issues easier and more productive. At the same time, for some KSAs you will be able to determine long-term objectives without going through the issue analysis process.

• *Critical Issue Analysis.* This is the same label as that used for the second element in tactical planning. The difference, once again, is related to scope and future impact. Critical issues in your long-range plan will address external opportunities and threats and internal strengths and limitations that will have a major effect on carrying out your mission and strategy and that will require more than one year to effectively resolve. Critical issues in your tactical plan will focus on the means of implementing the current year's portion of your long-range plan, improving aspects of your current plan that will be continued, and addressing short-term opportunities or problems that will impact your current year's results. For example, a critical strategic issue might be *projected obsolescence of high-volume, high-profit products/services.* A critical tactical issue might be *need to significantly improve our competitive position on [specific products/ services].* Critical strategic issues tend to be more opportunity oriented while critical tactical issues are generally focused more on problems.

- *Long-Term Objectives* (*LTOs*). These objectives represent the strategic positions you wish to reach at some designated time in the future. Objectives to be included in your tactical plan, conversely, will spell out the specific measurable results to be accomplished within the time span of your plan. LTOs frequently will begin with the phrase "to have" or "to become"—for example, *to have a minimum of 50 percent of our revenue generated by the year 2002 from products/services not currently being offered; or to become the largest supplier of [specified] services in our market by the year 2000; or to have a certified family counseling center that is financially self-sustaining by the year 2001*. By the way, this approach to long-range planning includes *financial projections* as a part of your LTOs rather than as a separate element. My experience in working with various client organizations suggests that all LTOs have financial implications and all financial projections are dependent on other LTOs. It makes sense therefore to include them together, so their interdependencies can be clearly established.

One of the other significant differences between long-term objectives and short-term tactical objectives is that LTOs can be established without necessarily knowing how you will reach them. In most circumstances, it's legitimate in long-range planning to set a position on the horizon that will make a major contribution to your mission and strategy and then to develop the means as you proceed. When you set tactical objectives, however, you had better have a well-thought-out action plan in mind or you are likely to have serious problems.

- *Strategic Action Plans* (*SAPs*). These plans identify major steps or milestones that are required to move you toward your long-term objectives. Particularly in the case of LTOs in which you are not certain how you will proceed, early stages of your SAPs will be related to evaluating the feasibility of various alternatives. SAPs typically will be multiyear and multifunctional. Portions will take place over a period of two or more years and will involve significant effort in more than one functional area such as marketing, development, and production. Consequently, SAPs for the entire organization are the primary bridges to your tactical plans and to long-range and tactical plans for functional departments that will be playing a role in meeting overall organizational goals.

• *Strategic plan review and modification*, while not an element of the plan, is a step you must go through both to validate the plans you have established and to make certain you have not overlooked anything significant.

One thing that will become obvious as you proceed with your long-range planning process is that it is iterative rather than linear. As you proceed through each of the four major elements, you may find it desirable or even necessary to refer back to earlier decisions, including some made as a part of your strategic thinking efforts, and reevaluate them in view of new insights. Planning is a dynamic, not a static, process. You need to be prepared to modify your plans and possibly change direction when circumstances justify.

How Does Our Long-Range Planning Support Our Strategic Thinking?

Individual strategic thinking involves the application of experience-based judgment to determine future directions. Organizational strategic thinking is the coordination of creative minds into a common *perspective* that enables the organization to proceed into the future in a manner fulfilling to everyone concerned.

The first book in this series focused on the articulation of your *values, mission, vision,* and *strategy*. Your mission statement is the single most important planning document to come out of this process. Properly developed, it will serve as a foundation for all major decisions that you and your management team will ever make. According to my definition, it encompasses the following major elements:

- The concept of your organization
- The nature of your business
- The reason your organization exists
- The customers you serve
- The principles and values under which you intend to operate

Following this approach, you design your mission statement to provide firm guidance in making important management decisions.

Conversely, you design your vision statement to inspire and motivate everyone who has a vested interest in your organization's future. Strategy addresses the direction in which your organization should be headed, its *driving force*, and other major factors that will help you determine what your future products and services should be and what markets hold the greatest potential. Vision and strategy may be included as a part of your mission statement, or they may be separate statements. Regardless of how it was arrived at, you need to have a mission statement both for your total organization and for that portion of the organization (division, department, unit) for which you are the accountable manager.

With the results of your strategic thinking in hand, you and your team should have a clear sense of direction that will help you identify critical strategic issues that need to be analyzed in order to produce long-term plans that will bring your strategic perspective to fruition. Long-range planning is the process that translates your dreams into reality. The future positions that come as a result of your long-range planning will become the tangible results that will make your strategic planning efforts a worthwhile investment.

How Does Our Long-Range Planning Support Our Tactical Planning?

Long-range planning is the bridge between your strategic thinking and the short-term performance you need to move you toward the future positions you have projected. Tactical planning gets down to the nitty gritty, spelling out what specific results you need in the immediate future and how your resources should be allocated. It is possible to do tactical planning without referring to a formal strategic plan, but performance will tend to be largely *reactive* to what is happening *now*. Having a clear sense of direction and some specific positions on the horizon will enable you to become much more *proactive* with your organization's performance while still being responsive to changing circumstances.

In Summary

Long-range planning is the middle component of the planning process, situated between strategic thinking and tactical planning. As such, it

- Helps you create the steps for carrying out your mission, vision, and strategy
- Focuses on looking at the horizon—where your organization needs to be at specific times in the future.
- Is a dynamic process that is flexible enough to allow and even encourage modification of plans in order to respond to changing circumstances.
- Incorporates four major elements:

    Key Strategic Areas, the major categories on which collective attention must be focused for the foreseeable future

    Critical Issue Analysis, a process of identifying, prioritizing, analyzing, and summarizing issues related to opportunities and threats that are external to your organization, and strengths and limitations that are internal to your organization

    Long-Term Objectives, which represent the strategic positions you wish to reach at some time in the future

Strategic Action Plans, the major steps or milestones required to move you toward the future positions you have projected

The next chapter will focus on the people who need to be involved in your long-range planning process and how they should approach their responsibilities.

CHAPTER TWO

Who Are Your Long-Range Planners?

It is axiomatic that the effectiveness of any planning process will be in direct proportion to the quality and quantity of effort put forth by the managers doing the planning. As with strategic thinking, long-range planning used to be considered almost exclusively the responsibility of top management. That is no longer the case. Almost every manager within an organization must of necessity look beyond the current year's efforts if the organization is to remain competitive. While the future direction of the total organization may come from the senior management team, managers throughout the organization will play a major role in determining the future positions to be pursued. Furthermore, they will be the primary implementers, the ones who will lead the effort to make the desired future a reality. My focus in this chapter is on the various roles that each level of management must play in the process, with particular emphasis on senior management, and on when and how to get others involved. (There will be considerable overlap between the content of this chapter and related chapters in *A Guide to Strategic Thinking* and *A Guide to Tactical Planning*. If you are already familiar with the approach recommended in either of those books, you may wish to skim this chapter, focusing on those portions directly related to long-range planning.)

What Is the Unit President Concept?

The Unit President concept has proven very useful in pinpointing responsibility for planning. Whether you are chief executive officer

(CEO) of your organization, a division or department head, a middle manager, a first-line supervisor, or an individual contributor within a larger unit, consider yourself president of a company. Consider everyone within the company with whom you must relate, even your boss, as your board of directors. The responsibility of a president is to clearly identify the future positions the organization must attain in order to satisfy the board and deliver the results that will ensure that attainment. As unit president, you need to make certain that your unit's future positions will at least be compatible with those of the entire organization. Once it is clear that they are, you will generally have a great deal of freedom in the way you manage your "company" as long as you produce the desired results. This principle and the rest of the contents of this book are equally applicable whether you function as a manager in private enterprise, government, or a not-for-profit organization. (While the Unit President concept will have more application in *tactical planning*, it's important to keep it in mind throughout the entire planning process.)

Who Does What in Long-Range Planning?

The ultimate responsibility for the development and implementation of the *total* organization's strategic and tactical plans lies with the CEO (or whoever is designated as your organization's key decision maker) and the senior team, which includes major department heads, one or two key staff advisers, and whoever will be guiding your planning process. If you are a member of the senior team, you are then responsible for seeing that the process cascades down through all levels under your leadership. This is true whether you are focusing on strategic thinking, long-range planning, or tactical planning. Let's look specifically at the roles of the key players in the long-range planning process.

   • The CEO must demonstrate strong leadership if the long-range planning process is to receive proper attention throughout the organization. This leadership includes being actively involved in the development process from the outset and allocating sufficient personal time for completion of assignments. Since long-range planning will lead to identification of the organization's key strategic areas, critical issues, long-term objectives, and strategic action plans, the results of these efforts must be ones the CEO can clearly and enthusiastically support. The CEO may at times be required to take a strong position while encouraging active involvement from others, to ensure that decisions are made and that the process does not become bogged down.

• *Senior management team members* function in dual roles. If you are a member of this team, you need to recognize that you serve as an extension of the office of the CEO. In theory, the CEO could complete the process independently. However, most executives recognize that they cannot do it alone, and the merging of divergent ideas will usually provide a stronger and more useful outcome. It needs to be clearly understood, however, that when you are working in this arena, you are representing the interests of the entire organization, not primarily those of your own function or program. Your second role, as indicated earlier, is to provide leadership in getting input from and communicating to others within your areas of responsibility.

• Members of the *board of directors* may be actively involved in the entire long-range planning process, or they may function primarily in a review and approval mode, depending on the board's size, structure, and level of interest. Board members of not-for-profit organizations, such as trade and professional associations, educational institutions, or community service agencies, frequently will be active participants in the development process either as a total body (if it is of a manageable size) or more frequently through a strategic planning committee (possibly the executive committee) that will do the initial development, followed by a review by the entire board. Most corporate boards, however, will look to the CEO and the senior management team for leadership in the initial determination of future positions toward which the organization should strive, while at the same time adding the wisdom of their experience in other organizations.

- The *planning coordinator* is someone within the organization who is designated as responsible for making sure that the entire planning process comes together. A member of the senior team, sometimes the CEO, typically assumes this role. The planning coordinator needs to be someone with good administrative skills who wants the responsibility. Whoever performs this role usually does so throughout the planning process to ensure continuity and may perform any or all of the following duties:

> Establishing and monitoring the planning schedule
>
> Coordinating and handling logistics of planning meetings
>
> Documenting and distributing meeting records

- The responsibilities of the *planning process facilitator* may be carried out by an internal or external coach/facilitator, preferably someone who does not have a strong personal vested interest in the outcome. Although a member of the senior team may have the skill to perform this role, he or she should not do so, because members of the senior team need to be free to take advocacy positions on certain issues and to express personal convictions during discussions. To be effective, the facilitator must remain neutral while guiding the discussion.

The planning process facilitator needs to have both the respect of participating executives and personal confidence, because it may be necessary at times to confront individual members of the planning team. An internal consultant brings an in-depth knowledge of the organization and generally is more accessible than an external consultant. An external consultant brings a broader and more diverse experience and is usually perceived as more neutral than an internal consultant. An effective internal/external consulting team brings the best of both worlds. Your planning process facilitator may perform any or all of the following duties:

> Designing or modifying the planning process
>
> Training/coaching managers involved in the planning process

Designing and facilitating planning meetings

Coaching/counseling your CEO

By adopting the Unit President concept, *other managers* are responsible for the determination of key strategic areas, critical issues, long-term objectives, and strategic action plans for their own units. Naturally, if such a process has been started by higher-level management, you will need to be certain that what comes out of your process is supportive of that of the total organization. If such a process has *not* been started at higher levels, you may still proceed with it at your level, using your best judgment to ensure that what comes out of your unit's efforts is at least compatible with where the rest of the organization appears to be headed.

How Much Time Is Required?

The amount of time required to complete the long-range planning component of the planning process will vary substantially depending on the size and complexity of your organization, the nature of your business, and whether you are starting from scratch or building on what has already taken place. If you already have satisfactory statements of your mission, vision, and strategy, my experience suggests that you can probably complete the bulk of your long-range plan in two two-day meetings held thirty to sixty days apart, *provided* that all members of your planning team have done their homework. If you have not yet completed your strategic thinking phase, you probably will need to hold another two-day meeting before your long-range planning meetings. You will at least need to review your mission, vision, and strategy statements for current relevance prior to embarking on your long-range planning efforts. The information and insights that are generated by the strategic thinking process will be extremely helpful as you proceed with the identification of your key strategic areas, analysis of your critical issues, determination of your long-term objectives, and preparation of your strategic action plans. Furthermore, by scheduling a series of meetings, with specific assignments in between, you will have an opportunity to get feedback on your initial efforts and make appropriate modifications as you proceed. You also need to recognize that each participating manager will have to invest several hours of individual preparation time to make the meetings as productive as possible.

Your initial long-range planning meeting will likely include either creation or review of your mission, vision, and strategy, and identification and prioritization of your key strategic areas and your potential critical strategic issues. You may also do an initial analysis of some of your critical issues and determine what additional information is needed (and who will be held accountable for getting it) in order to complete your analysis at a subsequent meeting. Your second two-day meeting (and a third one, if needed) will focus on completing your analysis of the critical strategic issues that need to be addressed in your plan as well as determining your long-term objectives and establishing your strategic action plans.

One thing to bear in mind if you are approaching this formally for the first time is that *you do not have to produce a complete strategic plan in your initial effort.* That could prove overwhelming. You might wish to concentrate initially on two or three critical issues that support your mission statement, with the expectation that you can expand on these and add others at a later time. In other words, you might use an incremental approach that will ensure you are making progress—much like a football team concentrating on making a series of first downs rather than going for a touchdown on every play.

How Do We Get Other Important Stakeholders Involved?

One of the key strengths of this process is that it provides an opportunity to involve others who have a vested interest in the outcome of your long-range planning efforts before, during, and after your initial development efforts. These "others" could include employees who may not be actively participating in the formulation process, customers, outside sales representatives, suppliers, strategic partners, community representatives, and perhaps even some of your competitors, if cooperative efforts could benefit all concerned. (This does not mean violating any antitrust restrictions, of course.)

Before

At the very least, you may wish to inform selected stakeholders that you are proceeding with the identification of your key strategic areas and critical strategic issues and invite them to share their thoughts informally. While many will not respond to such an invitation, at least they will be aware of what you are doing, and curiosity, if nothing else, is likely to keep them interested.

Other approaches to getting stakeholders involved include:

- Developing a brief series of questions, similar to those described in subsequent chapters, to be distributed to selected stakeholders for comment and returned prior to your initial meetings
- Conducting a series of focus group meetings designed to get their inputs on such questions.
- Appointing a task force composed of a cross-section of interested parties who can help highlight issues that need to be addressed

During

If you are scheduling a series of meetings, it may be appropriate for members of your planning team to meet with other people from their own units and perhaps from other units to get some interim feedback on the progress you are making. This is especially important as you complete your initial identification of critical strategic issues, to make certain you have not overlooked any issues that are especially important. (Subsequent chapters contain examples of the kinds of questions you may wish to ask.)

After

Once your planning team has agreed on your key strategic areas, critical issues, long-term objectives, and strategic action plans, it's important that you communicate them to those who will be most affected. In so doing, you may wish to point out that these analyses and plans are still subject to modification based on feedback received. Here are several ways in which you can communicate this information:

- Publish your completed strategic plan (the results of both your strategic thinking and your long-range planning efforts) together with any interpretation you may feel is necessary, as well as an indication regarding possible modification.

- Meet with representatives of various stakeholder groups (probably starting with employees) either individually or in small groups and discuss the implications of the results of your efforts for them individually and collectively as well as for the entire organization. My recommendation is that you circulate the materials either in advance of or during the meeting and *ask participants to interpret the meaning* of the documents rather than interpreting the documents for them. By doing so, you have a better chance of getting candid feedback on the clarity of your message.

- Circulate draft documents of the materials together with a series of feedback questions for people to react to. This method is especially useful in highly decentralized organizations or ones in which it would be difficult or too time-consuming to bring groups of people together for this purpose.

- Circulate the draft documents with a cover letter indicating that they will be reviewed and possibly modified at a designated future time, such as in six months.

The principle to keep in mind is that these materials need to be perceived as *living documents* that will be used in your tactical planning efforts as well as in ongoing decision making. They are not academic recordings to be filed and forgotten or ignored when it is convenient to do so. You can be sure that some of your stake-holders will challenge you when it is clear that your actions are not in line with positions taken in your strategic thinking or long-range planning efforts.

Can Long-Range Planning Be Used for Team Building?

My bias suggests that the entire planning process is one of the most powerful processes available for developing a sense of unity and mutual support among members of your management team, whether at the executive or unit level. My experience in working with a wide variety of organizations suggests that there is greater team-development value in having your team members go through this kind of exchange, in which they are focusing on the future of the organization, than there is in many of the purely interpersonal team development efforts that some of my colleagues advocate.

In Summary

- Long-range planning is a people process that needs all of your organization's key decision makers to be actively involved at various stages.
- The Unit President concept (you are president of your own "company" regardless of your position in your organization) is a useful way to pinpoint responsibility for planning.
- The ultimate responsibility for the development and imple-mentation of your organization's strategic and tactical plans lies with your CEO and the senior management team.
- A planning process facilitator who does not have a strong per-sonal vested interest in the outcome will help make your planning efforts more productive and objective.

- Long-range planning will require a modest investment of time spent in meetings with your key decision makers at both the total organization and unit levels; it may also require an investment of time in research and analysis to make these meetings as productive as possible.

- You do not have to produce a complete strategic plan in your initial effort; it can be developed incrementally.

- Other important stakeholders who may not be directly involved in your long-range planning process need to be given the opportunity to provide input before, during, and after your formal planning efforts in order to ensure their support as you proceed.

- Long-range planning is a powerful way to get the members of your management team involved in and committed to the future of your organization.

The first major element in the long-range planning process, key strategic areas, will be addressed in the next chapter.

CHAPTER THREE

What's Your Focus?

Determining Your Key Strategic Areas

Where do you start with your actual long-range planning? Do you throw ideas against the wall and see what sticks? Do you look at previous strategic plans and juggle the numbers? Do you review your tactical plans and see what factors have strategic implications? Do you examine your mission, vision, and strategy statements and focus on those portions that require specific long-term positions? Perhaps surprisingly, the answer is "all of the above." You will take advantage of whatever available sources will help you identify where you need to go.

Actually, your mission, vision, and strategy are probably the most productive initial stimuli. They help you focus on the concept and direction of your organization. The next step that many of my clients have found helpful is to determine their Key Strategic Areas (KSAs), categories in which critical issues can be identified and long-term objectives established.

What Are Key Strategic Areas and Why Are They Important?

Key Strategic Areas represent those major categories on which collective attention must be focused for the foreseeable future. As noted in Chapter One, some KSAs will look similar to Key Results Areas (KRAs), which are the equivalent step in the tactical planning process. KSAs, however, will be focused on the future, broader in scope than KRAs, and designed to help you determine where you want to be as an organization rather than the specific results you want to achieve. Reaching agreement on your KSAs will help you and your team

- Focus on those portions of your mission, vision, and strategy that need to be addressed in your long-range plan
- Identify and prioritize the critical strategic issues that represent your organization's strengths, limitations, opportunities, and threats as you proceed on your strategic journey
- Structure your long-range plan and, specifically, your long-term objectives into categories that will be easy to coordinate and track
- Form a bridge to the KRAs in your tactical plan to ensure that the steps in your strategic action plan are carried out in an effective and efficient manner

What Are Guidelines for Determining Our Key Strategic Areas?

The following basic guidelines can be used to help you determine KSAs for your total organization or your specific unit. A summary of these guidelines is provided in Figure 3.1.

1.   *They generally should identify those five to eight major categories within which your organization or your unit must establish future positions to be pursued.* Keeping your KSAs broad and relatively few in number makes it easier to concentrate your efforts on those that will have the greatest impact on where you need to be headed.

2.   *They should include both financial and nonfinancial areas.* Financial projections are an essential part of any long-range plan. You need to have a vision of what your future revenues, growth rates, profits, and net worth should be. These financial projections have little meaning, however, unless you also address issues and establish long-term objectives in such areas as future competencies, new products, and new or expanded markets.

3. *They should be focused on issues and future positions that require multiyear efforts.* Although some of your KSAs will be the same as the KRAs in your tactical plan, or similar to them, your KSAs should help you identify issues that cannot be effectively resolved during the coming year. Of course many of your KSAs will be a part of your long-range plan as long as your organization exists.

4. *They should directly or indirectly support your organization's mission, vision, and strategy statements.* Many portions of these statements can be converted directly into KSAs, while other portions will remain implicit. Where substantive changes are projected, you need to make certain that they will be addressed in one or more of your KSAs.

5. *They generally will require cross-functional effort.* At the total organizational level, most KSAs need the active participation of two or more major functions or organizational segments. KSAs for your unit should take into consideration such areas as new product/service development or customer relations, in which cooperation with other units is essential.

6. *Each KSA should be limited, generally, to two or three words and should not be measurable as stated but contain factors leading to future achievements.* Your KSAs should be specific enough to identify the kinds of issues and future positions on which you need to focus, but general enough to provide flexibility and, as appropriate, to identify more than one critical issue or long-term objective. Limiting your KSAs to short phrases makes it easier to determine where your attention needs to be directed.

Figure 3.2 contains several examples of KSAs that are appropriate to many organizations. This should not be seen as a prescriptive list, however. Some of the areas included will not apply to you, and undoubtedly there are other areas appropriate to your organization that do not appear here. The KSAs you select should be stated in terms that are relevant to you and others who must relate to them.

Figure 3.3 shows KSAs that are frequently used within specific organizational units. As you will note, some of these KSAs are identical to those identified as organizational KSAs; but the scope of the issues identified at the unit level is generally narrower than those focused on at the total organizational level. I have also included some KSAs that are more logically addressed at the unit level.

Figure 3.1 Guidelines for Determining Your Key Strategic Areas

---

1. They generally should identify those five to eight major categories within which your organization or your unit must establish future positions to be pursued.
2. They should include both financial and nonfinancial areas.
3. They should be focused on issues and future positions that require multiyear effort.
4. They should directly or indirectly support your organization's mission, vision, and strategy statements.
5. They generally will require cross-functional effort.
6. Each should be limited, generally, to two or three words and should not be measurable as stated but contain factors leading to future achievements.

Figure 3.2 Examples of Organizational Key Strategic Areas

Financial projections	Future customer satisfaction
Growth/diversification	Future products/services
Capital expansion	Future market positions
Future human competencies	Global expansion
Management succession	Future supplier development
Future production capability/capacity	Future strategic alliances
Future technology	Future legislative/regulatory impact
Research and development	Future service to industry
Future organizational structure	Future service to community

Figure 3.3 Examples of Unit Key Strategic Areas

Market penetration	Customer relations/satisfaction
Revenue/sales	Cost control/management
Future human competencies	Quality control/assurance
Employee development	Productivity
New product/service development	Process improvement
New/expanded market development	Production capability/capacity
Program/project management	Cross-functional integration
Technology	Supplier development/relations
Research and development	Unit structure

In Summary

Key Strategic Areas represent the categories in which critical strategic issues can be identified and long-term objectives established. Your KSAs will

- Be similar to Key Results Areas, the equivalent step in the tactical planning process; however, your KSAs will focus on the future and be broader in scope than KRAs, and they will be designed to help you determine where you want to be as an organization rather than to determine the specific results you want to achieve.

- Generally identify the five to eight major categories in which your organization or unit must establish future positions to be pursued.

- Include both financial and nonfinancial areas.

- Be focused on issues and future positions that require multi-year efforts.

- Be in direct or indirect support of your organization's mission, vision, and strategy statements.

- Generally require cross-functional effort.
- Be limited generally to two or three words, and they will not be measurable as stated but will contain factors leading to future achievements.

KSAs are a natural preliminary step toward identifying and analyzing your critical strategic issues, which will be addressed in the next chapter.

CHAPTER FOUR

What's Important?

Identifying and Analyzing Your
Critical Strategic Issues

Looking at what the future will bring is both exciting and a bit frightening. Can you really predict what the future will hold for you? Is there any way you can be reasonably sure that you are focusing on the factors that will have the best payoff? The answer to both questions is a qualified yes. This is where critical issue analysis comes in. Ironically, even though *analysis* is a key word in this phase of planning, you will still rely fairly heavily on managerial *intuition* in the process, substantially more so than when you are doing critical issue analysis in the tactical planning process. In looking ahead strategically, you will focus more on what you *think* is going to happen than on what you *know* is going to happen.

What Is Critical Issue Analysis and
Why Is It Important?

In strategic planning, critical issue analysis is an assessment of the major factors that are likely to influence how you carry out your organization's mission, vision, and strategy. It requires you to peer into your "crystal ball" and predict what you think is going to happen or needs to happen and what you must do to prepare yourself. The analysis process takes you beyond playing the role of swami, however, in that it disciplines you to look beyond predictions into validation, determination of possible reasons, and examination of various ways to address the issues you have identified. It forces you to look at both your external and internal worlds with a reasonably objective perspective. This process is addressed in what I refer to as a SLOTs Assessment. (No, we're not going to Las Vegas! SLOTs stands for "Strengths, Limitations, Opportunities, and Threats.") A SLOTs Assessment will help you identify the issues, opportunities, and challenges that need to be analyzed as you prepare your long-range plan. I will explain this assessment method in more detail shortly.

Your initial assessment is likely to identify far more potential critical issues than you can hope to address. Critical issue analysis is especially useful at this stage of the planning process because it will help you to

- Build an information base from which you can establish realistic long-term objectives and strategic action plans
- Validate or invalidate your assumptions about the future
- Focus on the vital few issues that will have the greatest impact on your organization's future
- Avoid premature decisions
- Reduce or eliminate the expenditure of resources (human and material) on low-potential issues
- Build your management team as a part of the decision-making process
- Fix accountability for actions that need to take place

How Does Critical Issue Analysis in Long-Range Planning Differ from Critical Issue Analysis in Tactical Planning?

While you will see similarities between the two processes, the primary differences relate to scope, breadth, and focus:

- Critical strategic analysis places much more emphasis on identifying and addressing future *opportunities* than on critical analysis of tactical issues, which tends to be more *problem* oriented.

- It focuses more on possible *reasons* than on possible *causes*, in order to more directly address opportunities.

- It frequently looks into the unknown or unexplored, while *tactical* analysis deals largely in familiar territory.

- It requires more creative thinking that focuses on what might be done rather than on what can or can't be done.

- It addresses issues that cannot be resolved effectively within one year.

- It is oriented more toward future *positions* than toward specific *results*.

- It will require more "what if" planning.

What Is a SLOTs Assessment?

You may be familiar with the term *SWOTs Analysis* as a part of strategic planning. (SWOTs refers to "Strengths, Weaknesses, Opportunities, and Threats.") I prefer SLOTs, substituting *limitations* for *weaknesses*, and I shall explain why shortly. *Strengths* and *limitations* are a part of your *internal* organizational world, where you can shape your future directly. *Opportunities* and *threats* take place in the world *external* to your organization, which you cannot control but which you may be able to influence and which you certainly can, and in fact must, plan for. The SLOTs Assessment process works equally well at both the organizational and the unit levels. I will be listing several generic examples in each of these categories. Of course, the items you identify should be specific to your own business.

- *Strengths* represent the major assets that you and your organization bring to the marketplace in four broad categories: human competencies, process capabilities (which includes facilities, equipment, and systems), products/services, and financial resources. Here are a few examples of *strengths* you might have in each of these:

Human competencies
    Innovative technical staff
    Skilled and experienced production staff
    Aggressive sales force
    Visibility in industry and community

Process capabilities
    Geographically dispersed facilities
    Relatively modern equipment
    Total quality system
    Quick responsiveness to customer concerns

Products/services
    Diversified product line
    Positive brand image
    Strong customer service
    Some customization

Financial status
    Strong cash reserves
    Excellent line of credit
    Reasonably good margins
    Employee stock ownership plan

• *Limitations* is my substitution for *weaknesses*. I don't like the term *weaknesses* because it implies there is something wrong with you, something that must be fixed; it sends negative value messages. I therefore prefer the term *limitations*, because there is less value judgment associated with it. My friend and colleague Joe Batten helped me to realize that a weakness is nothing more than a lack of a strength. If you have a limitation related to human competencies, process capability, or finances, you can strengthen it, or you can work around it so it doesn't impede your progress. Here are some examples of possible limitations in the four categories just identified:

Human competencies
    Inadequate research capability
    Lack of viable global sales staff

Need for multilingual engineers
Insufficient backups for executive staff

Process capabilities

Lack of outlet in Southeast Asia
Slow speed to market of new products
Need for additional raw material sources
Lack of timely information on consumer trends

Products/services

Overdependence on core products
Lack of competitive low-cost product line
Need for more customization
Need to segment products to niche markets

Financial

Insufficient R&D investment
Limited capital expansion funds
Pressure from owners for increased profits
Increasing margin pressure in core products

• *Opportunities* are events or circumstances that are likely to occur or that you might help to occur in your external world that could have a major positive impact on the future of your organization. These tend to appear in one or more of four broad categories: markets/customers, industry/government, competition, and technology.

In thinking about competition, you need to be aware that there are different kinds of competitive forces. Michael Porter, in his landmark book *Competitive Strategy*, identified five such forces. "The five competitive forces—entry, threat of substitution, bargaining power of buyers, bargaining power of suppliers, and rivalry among current suppliers—reflect the fact that competition in an industry goes well beyond the established players. Customers, suppliers, substitutes, and potential entrants are all 'competitors' to firms in the industry and may be more or less prominent depending on the particular circumstances. Competition in this broader sense might be termed *extended rivalry.*"[1] I encourage you to read Porter's book if you wish to explore competitive strategy in more depth. It's important to recognize these distinctions in competitive forces as you begin to identify potential critical issues.

Here are some possible opportunities you might have in each of the four broad categories:

Markets/customers
> Need for our products in Southeast Asia
> Virgin territory for our industry in China
> "Baby boomers" in or approaching their fifties
> Expanded use of Internet

Industry/government
> Increasing visibility of our industry
> Demand for controlled standards
> Market potential in new regulations
> Trade association marketing of industry

Competition
> Expansion of market potential by new entrants
> Financial overextension of some competitors (acquisition potential)
> Technical quality problems at some competitors
> High personnel turnover at some competitors

Technology
> Use of robotics to reduce costs
> Rapidly expanding state-of-the-art
> Increased availability of technical job shops
> Faster access to global markets

- *Threats* are events or circumstances that are likely to occur in your external world and that could have a major negative impact on the future of your organization. They tend to appear in the same four broad categories as opportunities. Ironically, with a creative approach many threats may be converted into opportunities. Those that cannot be converted may be minimized with careful planning. Visualize how you might convert some of the following threats into opportunities:

Markets/customers
> Reduction in size of major market segment
> Trade restrictions in specific foreign markets
> Consumers becoming more sophisticated
> Lack of consumer awareness of product value

Industry/government
> Emphasis on consumer risk protection
> Increased government controls
> Possible nationalization of industry in some countries
> Increased taxes, reduced deductions

Competition
> Price pressure from current competitors
> Current suppliers becoming competitors
> Current customers becoming competitors
> Emerging local competitors in foreign markets

Technology
> Some current products rendered obsolete
> Expensive retooling to use new technology
> Competitors' proprietary technology
> Unexpected side effects from technology

Your SLOTs Assessment will help you identify issues that might benefit from the process of critical issue analysis I will be illustrating later in this chapter.

How Do We Conduct a SLOTs Assessment?

Initially, the SLOTs Assessment will be primarily an intuitive process, although you are likely to reach a conclusion that you need more information as you begin identifying specific factors under each heading. I have found the most effective way to start is with a brainstorming effort involving members of the management team. While the examples identified here are primarily focused on factors that affect the entire organization, the process is equally applicable at the division, department, or unit level. You may also find conducting a SLOTs Assessment to be a useful exercise in your tactical planning, but its greatest benefit is related to identifying strategic issues.

1.   You need a skilled facilitator for this effort, preferably someone who does not have a vested interest in the outcome. The job of your facilitator is to keep you on track, to keep the process moving, to draw out the "quiet" members of your team, and to control those who tend to dominate.

2.   This assessment should be conducted early in your long-range planning effort, preferably at a location away from your organization's premises so that distractions will be minimized. It may either follow or precede your effort to identify your KSAs.

3.   My personal preference is to use two flipcharts for this exercise, although it could be done equally well using overhead transparencies, a whiteboard, or some of the more sophisticated computerized media. It's important that your entries remain visible to participants throughout the brainstorming exercise. This is one reason I like to use flipcharts, because they can be taped to the walls.

4.   I generally start with identification of the organization's strengths, encouraging participants initially to express their thoughts regardless of whether the ideas presented can be defended. An idea that is not defensible may trigger other ideas that are. Also, by focusing on strengths, the team tends to get into a "can do" frame of mind, which makes the rest of the brainstorming process easier and more effective. The only questions or discussion permitted during the initial effort are related to clarification of meaning.

5.   Next, we look at limitations, with the admonition that these do not necessarily represent weaknesses, but merely a lack of a strength. By reducing or eliminating the evaluative aspect, this

approach can become a productive way to obtain a realistic balance between strengths and limitations. In my experience, many organizations end up listing more strengths than limitations (which in itself signifies a healthy organization). Addressing strengths and limitations will help you determine how to take advantage of the potential opportunities you will discern shortly.

6.   At this point, I open the discussion of both lists and invite participants to talk about the merits or demerits of each of the items listed. We consolidate the ideas and eliminate any that clearly are not relevant. We do *not* attempt to address how to deal with them. That will come later, during the analysis phase. Our purpose at this stage is just to identify potential issues.

7.   The next step is to brainstorm potential opportunities using the four categories identified earlier. Opportunities represent your most important source of critical strategic issues. Encourage your team members to contribute ideas even if they have doubts about their validity. It's perfectly legitimate at this stage to speculate on what might occur that could be converted into an opportunity.

8.   Potential *threats* are identified next, once again using the four categories identified earlier. Some of your identified opportunities may also pose threats. As with opportunities, your team members should identify potential threats without being concerned about their legitimacy. It's a lot easier to eliminate inappropriate ideas during discussion than it is to add ones that might have been overlooked.

9.   Discussion of the lists of opportunities and threats should center on those ideas that are likely to have the greatest impact, positively or negatively, on the future of your organization. I encourage you to focus especially on threats that might be converted into opportunities. Once again, don't attempt to determine how to deal with any of the ideas at this point. Wait until you have prioritized your issues prior to analysis.

You should allow at least two hours for the entire brainstorming effort, and possibly as many as four hours. This effort will be a major means of identifying issues during this initial step in critical issue analysis. The same process may be applied at the unit level, although the entries will be narrower in focus.

What Is Involved in Critical Issue Analysis?

There are four primary steps:

1. *Identifying potential strategic issues.* A critical strategic issue is a current or anticipated event, situation, or trend that will have a major impact on carrying out your mission, vision, and strategy and that cannot be effectively resolved within one year. The first and most obvious step in the analysis process is to identify these issues. Your SLOTs Assessment will help you in this step. You need, however, to expand your thinking to determine if there are additional potential issues that may not have surfaced during that process. The same process may be applied to identifying critical strategic issues at the unit level. They will be narrower in focus, however, and directly related to your unit's roles and missions. Also, some of the issues you need to address in your unit may be referred to you from higher level management as a part of their critical issue analysis.

When a relatively large number of issues are identified, it may be useful to group them under their related KSAs in order to reduce overlap and to aid in prioritization.

2. *Prioritizing issues.* Determine the five to ten most important strategic issues—those that you perceive will have the greatest impact. Focusing on a limited number of truly vital issues makes it much more likely that those issues will receive the attention they deserve. Other identified issues need to be disposed of in some way, either by assigning them to specific units, deferring them for later review, or dropping them entirely.

3. *Analyzing issues.* This is the most crucial step in the analysis process. It involves both validating a particular issue and developing effective ways of addressing it. While some critical issues can be addressed to a considerable extent during the meeting in which they are first identified, most will require a significant amount of

additional research and analysis beyond the planning meeting, with reports given at a subsequent meeting. Accountability for this research and analysis needs to be accepted by a management team member before the initial meeting is adjourned. This team member becomes the *champion* for that particular issue, the one who will make certain it receives the attention it deserves.

4. *Summarizing issues.* After the research and analysis have been completed, the specific conclusions and alternative courses of action need to be summarized in a way that will make it easy to prepare your long-term objectives and strategic action plans.

These steps will be detailed further in the next section.

How Do We Complete Our Critical Issue Analysis?

1. *Identifying potential strategic issues.* As I have already discussed, the most effective way I have found to identify critical issues is through the SLOTs Assessment. Conducted properly, it should help identify most of the really critical issues. However, particularly in the opportunities area, it may prove necessary to do some additional research that could include market scanning, customer surveys, technological studies, current and potential competitor analysis, industry analysis, and a myriad of other research methodologies. (To retain the compact nature of this book, I do not describe these here. If you are interested, refer to the Annotated Resources section of this book, as well as to other books and periodicals that address the methodologies and techniques that interest you.)

As an alternative to the SLOTs Assessment, you may wish to ask the members of your planning team to complete a questionnaire either in advance of or during the first part of the initial long-range planning meeting. Individual responses to these questions may be shared and consolidated into a list of potential issues related to the total organization or to your specific unit. You might develop your own list of questions, such as:

- What are the five to ten most critical opportunities or challenges our organization (or unit) needs to address over the next five years? What impact will each of these issues have on the carrying out of our mission, vision, and strategy?

- What issues are likely to have the greatest effect on our long-term profitability and growth?

- What future positions related to markets/customers, industry/government, competition, technology, human competencies, process capabilities, products/services, or financial requirements need to be addressed?

- What data/information do you have or can you get that will help you validate and/or address these potential issues?

2. *Prioritizing issues.* Here is a simple but effective technique for identifying the five to ten most important issues that you should address or at least explore in order to carry out your mission, vision, and strategy:

- First, list your potential issues under the appropriate KSA. If more than one KSA applies, place the issue under the KSA with the greatest impact. Combine those issues that are clearly related, and eliminate any that are tactical (could be resolved within one year) or that are not significant. This should get your list down to a manageable size, say fifteen to twenty.

- Have each individual team member evaluate each of the remaining issues using an A-B-C weighting factor, with A being an issue that clearly must be addressed, B an issue where more information is needed before a decision can be made, and C an issue that could be referred to a specific department or unit, deferred for later consideration, or dropped without seriously impairing your long-range planning efforts. You may wish to limit the number of issues in each category (such as one-third in each). Figure 4.1 is a worksheet that can be used for this purpose.

- On a replica of Figure 4.1 that everyone can see, record the number of individual selections under each weighting factor.

- Compile a list of tentative priorities based on the number and nature of the responses. Where there is consensus that additional information is needed, write in the "What, Who, and When" column the information required, the name of the person accountable, and when the information will be provided. Figure 4.2 provides an example of a completed prioritization worksheet.

- Discuss the issues to ensure team agreement on the tentative priorities and determine when you will meet again to reach final agreement.

3. *Analyzing issues.* Some of the issues categorized as "A" may lend themselves immediately to group analysis in part or in whole. Other "A" issues as well as those selected as "B" issues may be more appropriately assigned to an individual team member to complete the data gathering and initial analysis separately and report back at a subsequent meeting when the team can address the issue more directly using the information presented. In either case, I have found the following format to be most useful in analyzing and discussing a specific issue:

- Using the worksheet provided in Figure 4.3 (page 44), write down the *potential/perceived issue*, keeping in mind that no issue is valid until data is generated to support it. As you proceed through your analysis, you may determine that the real issue you need to analyze is different from the perceived issue. For example, a perceived opportunity issue such as "need for our products in Southeast Asia" may turn out to be viable in only a few selected countries, such as Indonesia, Malaysia, and Thailand.

- Next, identify specific data or information that you either have or need to get in order to (1) validate or invalidate the potential/perceived issue as a real one, and (2) begin to identify ways to address the issue. The important distinction here

Figure 4.1 SLOTs Assessment Priorities Worksheet

	Weighting A	B	C	What, Who, and When
Strengths				
Limitations				
Opportunities				
Threats				

Figure 4.2 Sample Completed SLOTs Assessment Priorities Worksheet

	Weighting			What, Who, and When
	A	**B**	**C**	
Strengths				
Innovative technical staff	✓			
Aggressive sales force	✓			
Modern equipment		✓		Assess equipment, VP Mfg., 2/15
Total quality system			✓	
Positive brand image	✓			
Strong customer service	✓			
Strong cash reserves			✓	
Excellent line of credit			✓	
Limitations				
Lack of global sales staff		✓		Assess requirement, VP Sales, 2/15
Lack of executive backups	✓			
No Southeast Asia outlet	✓			
Speed to market too slow		✓		Analyze R&D flow, VP R&D, 2/15
Need for customization		✓		Assess market need, VP Mktg., 2/15
Need to segment products			✓	
Insufficient R&D investment			✓	
Increasing margin pressure			✓	
Opportunities				
Need for products in Southeast Asia	✓			
Expanded use of Internet		✓		
Industry more visible			✓	
Controlled standards		✓		
New entrants build market		✓		Assess potential impact, VP Mktg., 2/22
Competitors overextended		✓		
Use of robotics		✓		Assess potential, VP R&D, 2/22
Faster global access	✓			
Threats				
Market size reduction	✓			
Foreign trade restrictions		✓		
Increased government controls		✓		
Possible nationalization		✓		
Suppliers as competitors		✓		Assess potential, VP Mktg., 2/22
Customers as competitors		✓		Assess potential, VP Mktg., 2/22
Products become obsolete		✓		

is that the focus is on *data*, not opinion. What tangible evidence is there to justify investing time and other resources in addressing this issue?

- Next, assess the *possible reasons* why this is or might be a legitimate strategic issue for you. It's all right to use opinion here since hard data may not be available. Of course, an opinion backed by data is more useful. Assessment of strategic issues is focused on *reasons*, since many of these issues will be based on perceived opportunities. (Conversely, tactical planning will focus on *causes*, since more of those issues will be based on perceived problems.) For example, possible reasons for "need for our products in Southeast Asia" might be:

    Strong economic growth in targeted countries

    Relocation of some OEMs (original equipment manufacturers) in our industry to those countries

    Increasing demand for western-style products

    Potential for strategic alliance with company based in that region

- Next, draw one or more conclusions from your analysis that will help you focus on future positions you would like to attain, which will be reflected in your long-term objectives. For example, conclusions to the Southeast Asia issue might be:

    We have the potential to become a dominant supplier in our industry in Southeast Asian countries.

    We need to establish an outlet for our products and services in that region.

    A significant capital investment will be required if a manufacturing capability is placed in that region.

    A marketing and sales capability also will be required that both understands and has access to our target countries in that region.

- Since there normally are a variety of alternative ways of addressing an issue, explore as many possibilities as possible before settling on one or more specific approaches. Some alternatives to addressing the Southeast Asia issue might include:

   Focusing on one specific country, such as Malaysia, where the initial opportunity appears greatest

   Focusing on several target countries, such as Indonesia, Malaysia, and Thailand, that could be served from one location

   Creating a manufacturing operation or distribution center in one or more of the target countries

   Acquiring and converting an existing manufacturing operation or distribution center in the region

   Establishing a strategic alliance with a manufacturer, distributor, and/or marketing/sales organization in the region

   Retaining sales representatives in the region

- Finally, identify who will be the *champion* for this specific issue, the person who will produce additional required research and analysis and make certain that the issue continues to receive the attention it deserves.

4. *Summarizing issues.* Once you have completed your analysis, you need to determine which conclusions and alternatives have the greatest potential for effectively addressing your critical issue. You may be able to make these decisions based on the research and analysis you have already completed or you may need to go into substantially more detail, possibly to the extent of preparing a separate business plan (as in the Southeast Asia example) before you are ready to move on. Your summary of these decisions will provide you with a basis for establishing your long-term objectives and creating your strategic action plan.

Figure 4.3 Critical Strategic Issue Analysis

Potential/Perceived Issue:

Data/Information:

Possible Reasons:

Conclusion(s):

Alternative Ways to Address the Issue:

Champion:

Example of a Critical Strategic Issue
for the Total Organization

Several years ago I was consulting with a major hotel located in a popular resort area. At the time, it was the only hotel in that geographic area with its own convention center capable of handling meetings of up to 1500 attendees. A nearby hotel had just started construction of its own convention center that could handle a comparable-size group, and two other hotels in the area were actively exploring similar ventures. Initially, the hotel with which I was working viewed these developments as a *threat* to their market position—until they began to see them as an *opportunity* to open up their geographic area as a high-potential destination for major conventions involving several thousand attendees, which would create potential for added business for everyone. Consequently, they adopted a philosophy expressed by Cavett Robert, Chairman Emeritus of the National Speakers Association, when some of his colleagues expressed concern about new speakers "taking a piece of the pie." He said, "Let's not worry about that. Let's work together to build a bigger pie."

Figure 4.4 contains a highly condensed version of an application of the critical issue analysis process to the convention situation. I will not identify the hotels involved since I have taken several liberties with the example in order to illustrate the process.

How Can We Use Critical Issue Analysis
with a Department Strategic Project?

A growing biotechnology company was stalled in its expansion plans because of inadequate research capability. The vice president of research and development was charged with the responsibility for changing that situation. Figure 4.5 contains a condensed and edited version of how that department used the critical issue analysis process to address the situation.

The company eventually acquired a small laboratory in a different part of the country and hired a "name" scientist from a

Figure 4.4 Example of Critical Issue Analysis

Potential/Perceived Issue:

New entrants may expand market potential: "Let's build a bigger pie!"

Data/Information:

- Our hotel is the only one in our geographic area with facilities capable of handling conventions of up to 1500 attendees.
- X hotel has committed resources to developing a comparable convention capability.
- Y and Z hotels are actively investigating the potential of expanding their meeting facilities.
- We have received five inquiries in the past six months from organizations desiring convention facilities for more than 2000 attendees.
- There are at least fifty national and international trade associations that hold annual meetings attracting more than 5000 attendees.

Possible Reasons:

- Our area is known primarily as a vacation destination, and most promotional efforts by the Convention and Visitors Bureau, as well as by local hotels, have been focused on that reputation.
- Historically, hotels in our area have not cooperated in joint efforts to attract large conventions.
- Prior attempts to expand promotion of conventions, including possible development of a convention center, have met with strong resistance from local officials and the business community.
- Transportation and other related costs are perceived to be prohibitive for large conventions.

Conclusion:

We need to provide leadership as well as a substantial financial investment in developing our geographic area as a prime destination for large conventions. This will require active cooperation among the major hotels in our area, as well as among local officials, the business community, and the Convention and Visitors Bureau.

Alternative Ways to Address the Issue:

- Form a coalition with other hotels with similar interests.
- Strengthen the role of the Convention and Visitors Bureau.
- Promote the development of a convention center (which can be supplemented by hotel meeting facilities).
- Enlist the support of local officials and business leaders, emphasizing the economic, political, and other benefits to be gained from a major increase in large convention business, as well as the associated responsibilities.

Champion: General Manager

Figure 4.5 Example of Critical Issue Analysis with a Department Project

Potential/Perceived Issue:
Inadequate research capability

Data/Information:
- Our research laboratory has no room for expansion in its current location.
- We currently have four qualified research scientists on staff.
- Projected new product releases in our company's long-range plan require a minimum of seven to eight qualified research scientists.
- Two research scientists have left in the past year (one to go to a university, one to a competitor).
- Competitor X has released ten new products this year; we've released six.

Possible Reasons:
- Research laboratory facilities and equipment are inadequate.
- Qualified research scientists in our industry are in short supply.
- Competitors' compensation packages for research scientists are more attractive than ours.
- We lack a recognized "name" scientist on staff to attract others.
- Past company practice was to maintain a "lean and mean" staff.

Conclusions:
- We need to expand and improve our research laboratory. This will require additional, separate space.
- We need to actively recruit a minimum of three to four qualified research scientists during the next two years, including at least one recognized "name" in our industry. This will require reevaluation of compensation structure for current research staff as well as for candidates.

Alternative Ways to Address the Issue:
- Acquire an existing small research laboratory, including staff.
- Build or lease facility for new laboratory.
- Establish strategic alliance with an independent or university-based research laboratory.
- Retain a search firm to locate potential candidates.
- Develop creative compensation packages designed to attract the caliber of candidates we are seeking.

Champion: Vice President, Research and Development

university as its director, with a compensation package that included an equity position and the opportunity to pursue some independent research.

In Summary

- Identifying and analyzing your critical strategic issues is crucial to the effective development of your long-range plan. It provides you with the data and the rationale for setting strategic priorities, determining your long-term objectives, and preparing your strategic action plans.

- A SLOTs Assessment (which stands for "Strengths, Limitations, Opportunities, and Threats") will help you identify the issues, opportunities, and challenges that need to be analyzed as you prepare your long-range plans.

- A critical strategic issue is a current or anticipated event, situation, or trend that will have a major impact on carrying out your mission, vision, and strategy and that cannot be resolved effectively within one year.

- Limiting the number (between five and ten) of truly vital strategic issues will make it much more likely that those issues will receive the attention they deserve.

- The analysis process includes examining data/information (facts, not opinions) that either validate the issue or aid in addressing it; identifying possible reasons why it became an issue (may include opinions as well as facts); and reaching conclusions about the issue and addressing alternative ways to address it.

- Each critical issue that remains active needs a champion, someone who will carry out additional needed research and analysis and make certain that the issue continues to receive the attention it deserves.

- A summary of the conclusions and alternatives that have the greatest potential for effectively addressing your critical issue will serve as a basis for determining your long-term objectives and preparing your strategic action plans.

Having determined your KSAs and identified, prioritized, analyzed, and summarized your critical strategic issues, you are now ready to proceed to determining your long-term objectives, which is discussed in the next chapter.

Note

1. Michael E. Porter, *Competitive Strategy: Techniques for Analyzing Industries and Competitors* (New York: The Free Press, 1980), p. 6.

CHAPTER FIVE

What Should Be Your Future Positions?

Determining Your Long-Term Objectives

Long-term objectives are a way to document your dreams.

Dreams? You've got to be kidding! Objectives are supposed to be measurable and verifiable, and they should represent specific results to which we will be committed, right?

Sometimes, but not always! Long-term objectives represent the strategic positions you wish to reach at some designated point in the future. President Kennedy's decision in the early 1960s to, by the end of the decade, put a man on the moon and bring him back safely was a classic example of a strategic dream that captured the imagination of a nation and became an incredible reality.

What Are Long-Term Objectives and Why Are They Important?

Long-term objectives (LTOs) typically describe what your organization wants to have or become in the future, usually within three to five years (although your horizon may be longer than that in some instances). While they must have a degree of measurability, they will differ considerably from short-term or tactical objectives, as we shall see a bit later. They also include *financial projections*, since all LTOs have financial implications and all financial projections must be supported by other LTOs.

Reaching agreement on your LTOs will help you and your team:

- Focus your efforts on reaching those future positions that will enable you to carry out your mission, vision, and strategy
- Translate the conclusions from your critical issue analysis into meaningful targets
- Establish appropriate strategic action plans for reaching those targets, plans that can serve as a basis for determining some of your short-term objectives in your tactical plans
- Communicate your expectations to all important stakeholders (employees, customers, suppliers, owners)

How Do Long-Term Objectives Differ from Short-Term or Tactical Objectives?

LTOs represent future positions to be attained; short-term objectives specify measurable results to be accomplished within the time span of your tactical plan. LTOs also

- Are broad statements of intent that will produce many specific results
- Frequently represent what James C. Collins and Jerry I. Porras, in their book *Built to Last: Successful Habits of Visionary Companies*, refer to as BHAGs—Big Hairy Audacious Goals—which require extraordinary effort[1]
- Can be established without necessarily knowing how they will be reached
- Normally require cross-functional effort
- Normally do not identify cost factors

Where Do Long-Term Objectives Originate and How Are They Selected?

LTOs will evolve primarily through your KSAs and/or your critical issue analysis. Some long-term objectives will become obvious once your KSAs have been identified. Certain objectives may be dictated or strongly recommended by your board of directors, parent company, or other high-level body, while others may represent a decision that you and your team members have already made, in which case the writing of your LTO is a formalization of that decision. Here is a simple format for identifying your LTOs in this manner, followed by a few examples of LTOs that might be derived directly from your KSAs following this approach (Figure 5.3 at the end of the chapter contains a combined worksheet for listing LTOs related to KSAs):

1. Identify your key strategic areas that will require long-term objectives in order to carry out your mission, vision, and strategy. Limit these KSAs to a maximum of six to eight.

2. Identify within each KSA the potential future positions that will move your organization closer to fulfilling its mission, vision, and strategy. These are your potential LTOs.

3. Select the six to eight LTOs that will have the greatest impact on your future. As appropriate, write them in the format "To have (or become) [future position] by [year]."

Key Strategic Area	*Long-Term Objective*
Financial projections	To achieve $100 million in total revenue by [year]
	To achieve a minimum annual return on invested capital of 20 percent by [year]
Future market positions	To become the dominant supplier of [designated] products/services to the [designated] market by [year]
	To have at least 20 percent of revenue in [year] from markets not currently being served

Future technology	To have a separate research capability in [technology] by [year]
Future products/services	To have at least 20 percent of sales from new products (or services) by [year]
Global expansion	To become a multinational corporation with a minimum of 30 percent of net revenue coming from foreign sources by [year]

The other primary origination point for your LTOs is the process of critical issue analysis. Since there are no predetermined LTOs for your identified critical issues (otherwise there would be no need for the analysis process to take place), your conclusions and alternative ways of addressing each issue should provide you with most of what you need to determine future positions to be achieved. If the LTOs arrived at in this manner are to be included as a part of your strategic plan, you can add them in support of the appropriate KSA, following the format discussed earlier (and provided in Figure 5.3, page 60) and using your completed critical issue analysis worksheet (Figure 4.3) as backup information. If your critical issue is being analyzed on a project basis and will not be included as a formal part of your strategic plan, I recommend completing as your official document the worksheet provided in Figure 5.1, page 58.

Here are a few examples of LTOs that were determined as a result of critical issue analysis, followed by some examples of LTOs that might be appropriate to specific departments or units:

Organizational Long-Term Objectives

Critical Issue	*Long-Term Objective*
Need for our products in Southeast Asia	To have a profitable distribution center in Southeast Asia not later than [year]

New entrants may expand market potential	To have a minimum of five large conventions (excess of two thousand attendees each) booked by [year] as a result of collaborative activity with other hotels
Trade restrictions in specific foreign markets	To generate a minimum of $10 million in revenue in [country] by [year] as a result of a strategic alliance with a company based there

Department or Unit Long-Term Objectives

Critical Issue	*Long-Term Objective*
Need for more customization	To become a producer of customized products in at least 50 percent of our manufacturing operation by [year]
Expanded use of Internet	To have at least 20 percent of our revenue come as a result of Internet responses by [year]
Need for additional raw material sources	To have agreements with at least four additional sources of raw materials by [year]

How Do We Validate Our Long-Term Objectives?

As a final validation check of your LTOs, I recommend testing each statement against some or all of the following criteria:[2]

1. *Is it measurable or verifiable?* Will you and others affected be able to recognize the position when it is achieved? For example, an LTO "to become the dominant supplier" needs to be

measured by market share or other similar indicators. Also, information on the competition must be readily available.

2. *Is it achievable or feasible?* Even though your LTO needs to represent a significant challenge, there is no point in establishing one that is clearly beyond reach. What major efforts or critical changes must take place in order to attain that position? What is the likelihood of these changes happening? Answering these questions may require addressing such concerns as human competencies, financial resources, other priorities, impact of competition, or outside influences. It may be that the strategic action plan for a particular LTO needs to be developed before you can fully determine whether it is feasible or achievable (see the *decision tree* approach in Chapter Six).

3. *Is it flexible or adaptable?* Because a number of factors are unknown, whatever LTO you set must be flexible enough to take into account changing circumstances and new, related opportunities. For example, what you establish as a five-year objective may not necessarily be what is accomplished during that five-year period. As you go through the annual process of updating your long-range plan, your LTO may need to be modified to reflect up-to-date information.

4. *Is it consistent with the rest of your strategic plan?* Does this LTO move you closer to the positions that were taken as you constructed your mission, vision, and strategy?

The worksheet contained in Figure 5.3, page 60 includes the format described earlier and these validation questions.

Where Do Assumptions Fit?

While you may include some assumptions as a part of your critical issue analysis, you may find it useful to add something to LTOs that are based on assumptions over which your organization has little or no control. For example, the LTO "to become the dominant supplier" might be based on such assumptions as:

- There will be a continuing need for these services in those market segments as projected by industry statistics.

- There will be no major technological changes in the industry that could make the need for those services obsolete.

When your LTOs are based on assumptions, these assumptions should be included in your long-range plan. When your assumptions change, your LTOs must be reexamined and may have to be revised in light of new information.[3]

What Is an Appropriate Worksheet for Recording a Critical Issue and Resulting Long-Term Objectives?

There will be times when it is especially appropriate to trace a critical issue from identification through analysis to one or more LTOs and major actions in one worksheet. Such a worksheet can be used as supporting material for your strategic plan as well as to provide guidance to those who must work on it. It can be easily created by expanding the critical issue analysis worksheet introduced in Chapter Four (Figure 4.3), as shown in Figure 5.1. I have also included an example of a completed worksheet in Figure 5.2. Please note that "Major Actions" on this worksheet are intended only to identify significant events, not to include a complete strategic action plan, which will be described in Chapter Six.

Figure 5.1 Critical Issue Analysis and Plan

Potential/Perceived Issue:

Data/Information:

Possible Reasons:

Conclusion(s):

Alternative Ways to Address the Issue:

Champion:

Long-Term Objective(s):

Assumptions:

Major Actions:

Figure 5.2 Sample Completed Critical Issue Analysis and Plan

Potential/Perceived Issue:

Overdependence on core products

Data/Information:

- 83 percent of current revenue is generated by core products.
- Margins on core products have shrunk by 10 percent during the past year.
- We have lost 6 percent market share in core products in the past year to competitor X.
- Projected market demand in core products is expected to decline 7 percent annually for the next three years.
- Projected market demand for customized products is expected to increase 15 percent annually for the next three years.

Possible Reasons:

- We have been the dominant supplier of core products to our market for the past five years, leading to complacency on our part.
- New technology has created an increasing demand for products specifically customized to our customers' requirements.
- We have lagged behind competitor X in converting some of our manufacturing operations to customized operations using new technology.
- Most members of our sales force are not sufficiently knowledgeable about new technology to effectively sell customized products.
- Sales commissions are the same for customized products as for core products.

Conclusions:

- We must significantly increase our sales of customized products while maintaining our market share in core products.
- We need to convert a significant portion of our manufacturing operations to handle customized products. This will require an investment in new equipment and retooling of some existing equipment.

Alternative Ways to Address the Issue:

- Reduce commissions on core products.
- Increase commissions or add incentives for sales of customized products.
- Train existing sales staff in new technology and methods of selling customized products.
- Hire new sales staff with the knowledge and skills necessary to sell customized products.
- Retain outside sales representatives to sell customized products.
- Convert manufacturing operations in Building C to handle customized products exclusively.
- Convert all manufacturing operations to handle both customized and core products.
- Acquire a small manufacturing company with the capability of producing customized products.

Champions: Vice President, Sales, and Vice President, Manufacturing

Long-Term Objectives:

- To have a minimum of 55 percent of sales revenue from customized products by [year].
- To become a producer of customized products in at least 50 percent of our manufacturing operation by [year].

Assumptions:

- Market demand for core products and customized products will remain consistent with our projections.
- No additional major competitors will enter our industry during the next three years.

Major Actions:

- Conversion of Building C to customized manufacturing operation
- Change in compensation structure to incentivize customized product sales
- Training of sales staff in new technology

Figure 5.3 Long-Term Objectives Formulation Worksheet

1. Identify your key strategic areas that will require long-term objectives in order to carry out your mission, vision, and strategy. Limit these KSAs to a maximum of six to eight.

2. Identify within each KSA the potential future positions that will move your organization closer to fulfilling its mission, vision, and strategy. These are your potential LTOs.

3. Select the six to eight LTOs that will have the greatest impact on your future. As appropriate, write them in the format "To have (or become) [future position] by [year]."

Key Strategic Area   **Long-Term Objective**

Questions for Validating Your Long-Term Objectives

Is it measurable or verifiable?

Is it achievable or feasible?

Is it flexible or adaptable?

Is it consistent with the rest of your strategic plan?

In Summary

- Long-term objectives represent the strategic positions you wish to reach at some designated point in the future.

- They include financial projections, since all LTOs have financial implications and all financial projections must be supported by other LTOs.

- LTOs can be established without necessarily knowing how they will be reached.

- LTOs may be derived directly from your key strategic areas, or through the process of critical issue analysis.

LTOs define what you would like to have or become in the future. Strategic action plans, the subject of the next chapter, will help you lay out a road map for reaching each of these future positions.

Notes

1. James C. Collins and Jerry I. Porras, *Built to Last: Successful Habits of Visionary Companies* (New York: HarperCollins, 1994), p. 8.
2. Adapted from Patrick J. Below, George L. Morrisey, and Betty L. Acomb, *The Executive Guide to Strategic Planning* (San Francisco: Jossey-Bass, 1987), pp. 71–73.
3. Adapted from Below, Morrisey, and Acomb, *The Executive Guide to Strategic Planning,* pp. 71–73.

CHAPTER SIX

How Will You Reach Your Future Positions?

Preparing Your Strategic Action Plans

Your long-term objectives identify where you want to be at some point in the future. As with any journey, you start by identifying your destination and desired time of arrival. But that's not enough! You still need to determine what mode of transportation and what route will be most appropriate to ensure your arrival at your destination on time and in condition to enjoy your stay. You also need to be alert to such things as weather, road conditions, and either expected or unexpected events that may make detours, delays, or even accelerations a reality. This is where your Strategic Action Plan comes into play.

It became apparent early in the planning stages of implementing President Kennedy's decision to put a man on the moon that it would not be practical to have the Apollo command module land on the moon and then attempt to launch it back to earth once the landing mission was completed. This realization led to the design and construction of the Lunar Excursion Module (LEM), a smaller and lighter vehicle in which two astronauts could descend to the moon's surface, complete their exploration assignment, and launch from the moon's surface to rejoin the Apollo module in orbit prior to their return journey to earth. That development was part of a monumental Strategic Action Plan.

What Are Strategic Action Plans and Why Are They Important?

Strategic Action Plans (SAPs) identify the major events, phases, or accomplishments that have to take place if you are to attain your

LTOs. They do not represent a detailed step-by-step procedure; rather, they focus on critical milestones that need to be achieved during the life of the plan, and specify accountability for the plan's completion. Reaching agreement on your SAPs will help you and your team

- Validate or invalidate the feasibility of achieving your LTOs, including the need for modification of your LTO or SAP when appropriate
- Assure that the major steps in your SAP will be addressed in sufficient time and with sufficient resources
- Determine where cross-functional linkages must occur
- Form a bridge to your short-term tactical objectives and action plans
- Communicate your expectations to those who must contribute to your efforts, to enable them to prepare their own related action plans
- Establish a basis for reviewing progress toward achieving your LTOs and taking corrective action when required

How Do Strategic Action Plans Differ from Tactical Action Plans?

Your Strategic Action Plans will look similar to your tactical plans in some respects. However, your SAPs are intended to identify major milestones, while your tactical action plans will deal with specific short-term activities or events. The steps in your SAP

- Will be broad statements that can be broken down by the accountable person into detailed plans as needed
- Need to explore various options and provide for contingency plans as appropriate
- Will identify both capital and operating resources as necessary

- Generally will focus on broad time frames (specific year or quarter) rather than on specific target dates for step completion
- Will include both primary and supporting accountability

What Are Decision Trees and How Are They Used in Long-Range Planning?

Because of the complex nature as well as the extended time requirements associated with many of your SAPs, you may not be able to specifically identify some of the events or accomplishments needed until you are well into implementation of the plan itself. You may be considering several options with which you will need to experiment before determining which option or combination will provide you with the best results, or you may not be sure that your plan will work at all until you have completed a particular phase, such as a market analysis or a production feasibility study. In any of these circumstances, you need to establish *decision points*, when you will determine whether to continue on your current course, redirect your efforts to one or more different courses, or redefine or abort your plan because it cannot be completed as currently structured. A *decision tree*, as conceptualized in Figure 6.1, is a way to graphically illustrate your dilemma, to identify specific *decision points* where you will make *go*, *modify*, or *no-go* decisions. A decision tree can also help avoid premature closure on an issue. It can leave a decision open until more information is available on how the plan is working.

For example, as shown in Figure 6.2, if your LTO is "to have a profitable distribution center in Southeast Asia not later than [year]," you may wish to conduct a combination market and feasibility study to determine which country or countries have the greatest potential for initial market penetration as well as a physical location for your center. At your first decision point, therefore, you may discern that Indonesia, Malaysia, and Thailand are all viable

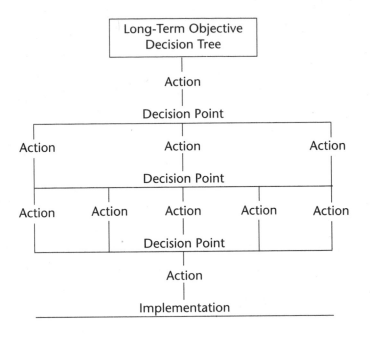

Figure 6.1 Decision Tree Model

candidates. Your next step may be to explore each of these countries individually in terms of access to markets, possible locations, availability of potential employees, acquisitions and/or strategic alliances, local restrictions or regulations, and start-up and operating cost estimates. At your next decision point, the results of your research may indicate that Indonesia, specifically Jakarta, presents more favorable factors than either Malaysia or Thailand. From there, you may need to evaluate whether to proceed with leasing, acquiring, or building an appropriate facility, licensing a local manufacturer's representative, establishing a strategic alliance with an Indonesian company, hiring local management, or assigning current company staff to manage the operation. This *decision point* may lead you to conclude that a strategic alliance with an Indonesian company is your most practical alternative.

It may take you several months to come to this third decision point. You may even reach the conclusion that the timing is not right, that your first choice for a strategic alliance will not be pre-

Figure 6.2 Decision Tree Example

pared to join forces with you until next year, or that the potential is not as great as you predicted. This realization could lead to a decision to postpone action or even to abort the entire plan. While economically painful, the cost of aborting at this stage is considerably less than the cost associated with shutting down a failed venture. Conversely, if each of your decisions has been positive to this point, you can revise your LTO to read "to have a profitable distribution center serving Southeast Asia, based in Jakarta, not later than [year]" and then proceed with the rest of your SAP to make that intention a reality.

How Do We Prepare Our Strategic Action Plans?

Figure 6.3 provides a recommended format for laying out your SAP. It identifies the elements that have to be addressed. While it looks very similar to the format that will be recommended for use in a tactical action plan, its scope is considerably broader. As with any planning process, feel free to adapt this format to suit your need.

1. *Major events, phases, accomplishments.* Identify the principal milestones that must be passed in order to stay on track toward reaching your LTO. If using a decision tree approach is appropriate as part of your SAP, each decision point becomes one of your early milestones. Typical steps in major new product development, for example, include market research and analysis, technical research and analysis, design, prototype development, prototype testing, pilot run, market testing, production implementation, marketing, sales, and service. Note that each of these steps will require a detailed action plan of its own, developed by the accountable person or department, before it can be carried out. In most cases, it is not appropriate to include that amount of detail in your SAP.

2. *Primary and supporting accountability.* An individual person, department, or unit needs to be charged with the primary accountability for seeing that each step in your SAP is carried out. (If a department or unit is so identified, its designated head is the accountable person by default.) Other individuals, departments, or units who will be making significant contributions are identified in the *supporting* column. *Primary* accountability includes whatever coordination may be required to ensure that supporting contributions are made.

3. *Schedule.* The schedule includes when the particular step must be started, completed, or both. While there will be exceptions, using a time frame such as a specific quarter is acceptable in most SAPs. Since the start or completion of some steps will be dependent upon or heavily influenced by what happens in other steps, you will need to allow flexibility in your schedule and be prepared to make modifications (and communicate them) when necessary.

4. *Resources. Capital* will include such things as acquisitions, facilities, major equipment, or other investments not covered in normal operating expenses. *Operating* resources are all of the ongoing resources required to support this action step, whether or not they are included in your current budget. *Human* resources include

Long-Term Objective:

| Major Events, Phases, Accomplishments | Accountability | | Schedule | | Resources | | | Feedback Mechanisms |
	Primary	Supporting	Start	Complete	Capital	Operating	Human	

Figure 6.3 Strategic Action Plan Format

the types and, if possible to determine, the quantity of specific human competencies needed to support this step. While the human resources needed may be covered under your operating resources, it's especially important to identify them if they are highly skilled or in short supply.

5. *Feedback mechanisms.* Identify how the person with primary accountability will keep others who need to know informed of progress. Feedback mechanisms could range from a sophisticated computerized tracking system to a simple chart to a verbal or written report. (I will cover this element in more detail in Chapter Seven.)

What Are Some Examples of Strategic Action Plans?

Figures 6.4 and 6.5, pages 72 and 73 contain examples of SAPs that support the LTOs identified in Figure 5.2. One example is focused at the total organization level and the other is focused at the department or unit level. Notice both the similarities and the differences between them. Recognize also that these examples are intended as illustrations and will not necessarily be applicable to your specific situation.

How Do We Establish a Bridge to Our Tactical Plans?

Let's assume for the moment that your long-range plan has a three- to five-year horizon. Each of the SAPs you have developed in support of your LTOs will contain major events, phases, or accomplishments that must be completed at some point within that time frame. Some of the effort required may occur during only one of the plan years covered in that period, while other effort may extend over two or more of the plan years. It's essential, therefore, that you have your long-range plan and, in particular, your Strategic Action Plan available as you prepare your tactical plans. Every step in your SAP needs either to be converted into an objective or to be made a part of an action plan within your tactical plan. For example, notice that step one in Figure 6.4, "complete market study on sales potential for customized products," must become an objective for year one, second quarter, in the marketing department's tactical plan. One of the added values of referring to your SAP is that doing so provides one more opportunity to validate, modify, or invalidate the strategic journey on which you are proceeding.

Long-Term Objective: To have a minimum of 55 percent of sales revenue from customized products by [year].

Major Events, Phases, Accomplishments	Accountability		Schedule		Resources			Feedback Mechanisms
	Primary	Supporting	Start	Complete	Capital	Operating	Human	
1. Complete market study on sales potential for customized products	VP Marketing	VP Sales	Year 1 Q1	Year 1 Q2		$10,000	500 hrs.	Written progress reports
2. Revise sales forecasts for Years 1, 2, and 3 to reflect changes	VP Sales	VP Marketing	Year 1 Q2	Year 1 Q2			50 hrs.	Revised forecasts
3. Convert Building C to customized manufacturing operation	VP Mfg.	VP Engineering VP Administration	Year 1 Q2	Year 2 Q4	$500,000	$80,000	1100 hrs.	Written progress reports
4. Change compensation structure to incentivize customized sales	VP HR	VP Sales	Year 1 Q3	Year 1 Q4		$50,000	100 hrs.	Revised structure report
5. Train sales staff in new technology	Director of Training	VP Sales	Y2, Q1	Y2, Q2		$50,000	1000 hrs.	Training plan reports
6. Expand production of customized products – to 25 percent – to 30 percent – to 40 percent – to 50 to 55 percent	VP Mfg.	VP Engineering	Y1, Q4	Y2, Q4 Y2, Q4 Y3, Q2 Y3, Q4		Budgeted	Budgeted	Production reports
7. Increase sales of customized products – to 25 percent – to 30 percent – to 40 percent – to 55 percent	VP Sales	VP Marketing	Y1, Q4	Y2, Q2 Y2, Q4 Y3, Q2 Y3, Q4				Sales reports
8. Revise sales forecasts	VP Sales	VP Marketing		Y3, Q4				Revised forecasts

Figure 6.4 Sample Strategic Action Plan

Long-Term Objective: To convert Building C to customized manufacturing operation by [year].

Major Events, Phases, Accomplishments	Accountability		Schedule		Resources			Feedback Mechanisms
	Primary	Supporting	Start	Complete	Capital	Operating	Human	
1. Complete feasibility study on conversion requirements	VP Engineering	VP Manufacturing	Year 1 Q1	Year 1 Q2		$10,000	100 hrs.	Written progress reports
2. Complete converted production line design and equipment specifications	VP Engineering	VP Manufacturing		Year 1 Q3		$50,000	500 hrs.	Design review meetings
3. Purchase and install new equipment	Purchasing	VP Manufacturing	Y1, Q3	Y1, Q4	$400,000		100 hrs.	Written progress reports
4. Modify existing equipment	VP Mfg.	VP Engineering	Y1, Q3	Y1, Q4	$100,000	$10,000	100 hrs.	Written progress reports
5. Train production staff	Director of Training	VP Manufacturing	Y1, Q3	Y1, Q4		$10,000	300 hrs.	Training plan reports
6. Initiate customized production line	VP Mfg.	VP Engineering				Budgeted	Budgeted	Production reports
7. Increase production of customized - to 25 percent - to 30 percent - to 40 percent - to 50 to 55 percent	VP Mfg.	VP Engineering	Y1, Q4	Y2, Q2 Y2, Q4 Y3, Q2 Y3, Q4		Budgeted	Budgeted	Production reports
8. Reassess future production capacity	VP Mfg.	VP Engineering		Y3, Q4				Production forecast

Figure 6.5 Sample Department Strategic Action Plan

In Summary

- Strategic Action Plans identify the principal milestones that must be passed to stay on track toward reaching your LTOs.

- SAPs do not represent a detailed step-by-step procedure; rather, they focus on critical milestones that need to be achieved during the life of the plan.

- A decision tree will help you identify specific points in your SAP where you will make go, modify, or no-go decisions; it is especially helpful when you do not have all the information you need prior to preparing your SAP.

- Your SAPs include

  Major events, phases, and accomplishments

  Primary and supporting accountability for each step

  A schedule (when each step must be started, completed, or both)

  Resources (the capital, operating, and human resources required to carry out each step)

  Feedback mechanisms (how and when those with a need to know will be kept informed of progress)

- Your SAPs will be the primary bridge between your strategic and tactical plans, providing the information necessary to establish your short-term objectives and action plans.

- Your SAPs provide one more opportunity for validating, modifying, or invalidating the strategic journey on which you are proceeding.

The next chapter focuses specifically on reviewing and modifying your total strategic plan so that it keeps pace with changing circumstances.

CHAPTER SEVEN

How Will You Know Where You Are?

Reviewing and Modifying Your Strategic Plan

You will notice that the subtitle of this chapter is "Reviewing and Modifying Your Strategic Plan," not reviewing and modifying your long-range plan. Although the emphasis in this book has been on long-range planning, and although you will probably focus far more on your long-range plan in your review process, your reviews need to be conducted within the context of your total strategic plan, which includes strategic thinking (articulating your mission, vision, and strategy), which was covered in the first book in this series. One of the failings of many strategic planning efforts is the tendency to complete the strategic plan as an *event,* then to put it on the shelf and forget about it until someone asks about it or it is time to do the plan again. My experience suggests that the success of any plan's implementation (strategic, tactical, or otherwise) is in direct proportion to the thoroughness of the plan review process. While you may not find it necessary to formally review your strategic plan as often or as thoroughly as you will review your tactical plan, I firmly believe you need to take a look at it in its entirety on a regularly scheduled basis or whenever a change in strategic direction is contemplated.

What Is Strategic Plan Review and Why Is It Important?

Strategic plan review requires you and your team to examine your entire strategic plan periodically (my recommendation is at least once a quarter), to make certain that everyone is still pulling in the same direction. Regular strategic plan review will help you and your team

- Keep your mission, vision, and strategy fresh in your minds
- Make certain your day-to-day activities are consistent with and supportive of your mission, vision, and strategy
- Identify circumstances (such as a technological breakthrough) that may require you to reassess and possibly change your strategic direction
- Focus on aspects of your long-range plan that need to be addressed immediately or in the near future
- Ensure that those portions of your tactical plan that are directly related to your long-range plan are being implemented in a timely and effective manner
- Identify new information that needs to be included in your critical issue analysis, particularly information that may lead to modifications in some of your LTOs and/or SAPs
- Remember that planning is an ongoing *process*, not an *event*

How Does Strategic Plan Review Differ from Tactical Plan Review?

While I recommend that you formally review your strategic plan at least once a quarter, I am adamant about the necessity of formally reviewing your tactical plan quarterly and in some cases more frequently. Tactical plan review will be thoroughly discussed in Chapter Eight of the third book in this series, but for purposes of comparison here, note that generally your tactical plan review will

- Require more detailed study than your strategic plan review
- Take longer than your strategic plan review (unless significant changes are required in your strategic plan)
- Lead more frequently to specific short-term corrective action and/or plan modifications

- Focus on three perspectives:

    What is going right and what you can learn from that

    What is not going right and what you are doing about it

    What is different from what existed at the time the plan was created (which may require an immediate plan modification)

- Involve more people than your strategic plan review

When and How Do We Conduct Our Strategic Plan Review?

There are four primary occasions for this review. The first is the *periodic progress review* (which has been my focus in this chapter thus far). The second occasion is an *ongoing selective review* of specific portions of your long-range plan that may require attention. The third review occurs on an ad hoc basis whenever a *change in strategic direction* is necessary or being contemplated. The fourth review typically takes place once a year at the *start of your planning cycle*. I will address each of these separately.

1.   *Periodic progress reviews* of your strategic plan need to occur on a *scheduled* basis. My observation is that if progress reviews are not entered on the calendar as official management meetings, they are not likely to take place as often as they should. If you have regularly scheduled staff meetings, you may wish to make strategic plan review an agenda item on the last such meeting of each quarter throughout the year. If you have regularly scheduled tactical plan review meetings, you may wish to review your strategic plan as a preliminary step at some or even all such meetings. Some management teams find it more productive to schedule their strategic plan reviews separately from their tactical plan reviews, such as on the first Friday of each quarter, limiting their discussion to strategic issues. A strategic plan progress review usually can be completed within one or two hours unless significant changes are anticipated.

Although you may wish to alter your approach periodically to keep your review meeting from becoming humdrum, here is an agenda that some management teams have found useful:

- *Mission/vision review:* review by a different management team member at each meeting, who gives a brief update on how the mission/vision are being interpreted or used in his or her area of responsibility
- *Strategy review:* review by another team member, with a similar update on interpretation and use
- *KSA and LTO review:* quick overview of KSAs and LTOs by entire team to keep KSAs and LTOs in focus
- *Critical issue review:* quick overview of all identified critical issues to make certain they are still valid and to identify any others that should be considered
- *Selected critical issue, LTO, and SAP review:* report on progress of two or three critical issues by the issue champions
- *Agreement on next steps:* what is to take place before the next plan review meeting; agreement on a date for the next meeting if not already scheduled

2.   *Ongoing selective review* of portions of your long-range plan that may require attention should take place as needed. Ways of keeping track of your strategic or tactical plans (which also may be used as feedback mechanisms in your SAPs) include:

- *Status reports,* whether given verbally, electronically, or in writing. My recommendation is that written status reports be *brief* (one or two pages), in *outline* rather than narrative form, and structured to quickly *highlight* the most critical information. Standardized reporting formats, which can be either manually or electronically generated, can be very useful in keeping such reports from becoming overly time-consuming for either the generator or the receiver.

- *Visual displays* such as line or bar graphs, milestone charts, and problem-oriented charts that are updated on a regular basis can be very effective in providing motivation as well as instant visibility. To be truly effective, such displays must show projections that reflect probable reality rather than straight-line averaging (since most factors don't operate on a straight line), and they must instantly highlight variances requiring corrective action without a complicated interpretation. There are many simple yet sophisticated software programs that can help you do this.

3.   At the risk of belaboring the obvious, you must review and be prepared to modify your strategic plan any time a *change in strategic direction* is either planned or being contemplated. Such changes could be dictated by a merger; an acquisition; a new mandate from your owners, parent organization, or higher-level management; or a new business opportunity that falls outside your current strategic plan. 'Nuff said!

4.   When you are approaching the *start of your planning cycle*, it is a natural time to review where you are in your current strategic plan. This review will help you determine whether you need to create a whole new plan or if an extension or modification of your existing plan, sometimes referred to as a *rolling* plan, is appropriate. At the very least, I recommend that you go through the critical issue identification process to determine if some of your issues either are resolved or have become less critical and, what is more important, to see if other critical issues have emerged.

Why, When, and How Do We Modify Our Strategic Plan?

I will confine my suggestions here to modifications you might wish to make in your long-range plan, particularly your LTOs and SAPs. Naturally, you will make appropriate changes to your mission, vision, or strategy if changing circumstances make such modifications necessary. Here are a few examples of why changes to portions of your long-range plan might be appropriate:

- Technological breakthroughs
- Unanticipated business opportunities
- Unanticipated competition
- Downturn or upturn in the economy
- Political changes
- New or expanded major contract
- Loss of major contract
- Loss of major supplier
- Lack of adequate capital resources
- Unanticipated availability or loss of key personnel

Long-range plans should be changed only after careful deliberation determines that such modifications are clearly justified. Remember, any substantial changes to your LTOs or SAPs are likely to have ripple effects that will impact other plans and other parts of the organization. If such a change is called for, however, you need to make it quickly, taking into consideration what and who will be impacted. You may be able to make the necessary modifications to your LTO and/or SAP quite easily as an individual or in a team meeting, or you may find it useful to go through the critical issue analysis process again, factoring in the changing circumstances. Finally, any changes you make need to be communicated quickly and thoroughly to everyone affected so they can make whatever adjustments may be required in their plans.

In Summary

- You need to periodically review and modify, as appropriate, your entire strategic plan, including the results of your strategic thinking (mission, vision, and strategy) as well as of your long-range planning effort.

- There are four primary occasions for this review:

  Periodic progress reports, scheduled at least once each quarter

  Ongoing selective review of portions of your long-range plan that may need attention

  Ad hoc reviews whenever a change in strategic direction is either planned or being contemplated

  Annual reviews when you are approaching the start of your planning cycle

- Long-range plans should be changed only after careful deliberation determines that such modifications are clearly justified because of the potential impact on other plans or on other parts of the organization.

This completes our discussion of all the elements of the long-range planning process, including some thoughts on reviewing and modifying your entire strategic plan. The next and final chapter will help you to assess where you are now in your strategic planning process and provide you with a methodology for moving ahead.

CHAPTER EIGHT

How Does Your Strategic Plan Come Together?

The completion of your long-range plan along with the results of your strategic thinking comprise the visionary, future-oriented part of your planning process. Combined, they make up your organization's or unit's strategic plan. Your strategic plan provides the framework from which your tactical plans can be developed and implemented, leading you on your strategic journey. Ironically, you can implement your tactical plans without a strategic plan, but you *cannot* implement your strategic plan without a tactical plan. This does not make either plan more important than the other. It does illustrate the concept of synergy, however, because the results of your planning efforts will be much more effective when all three components of your planning process—strategic thinking, long-range planning, and tactical planning—are integrated in such a way that each feeds on the other, as illustrated in Figure 8.1. Bear in mind once again that

> *Strategic thinking* leads to *perspective*
> *Long-range planning* leads to *position*
> *Tactical planning* leads to *performance*

What Goes into Our Strategic Plan?

A complete strategic plan includes the results of your strategic thinking and your long-range planning. Your strategic plan may not necessarily contain all the elements shown in Figure 8.1, however.

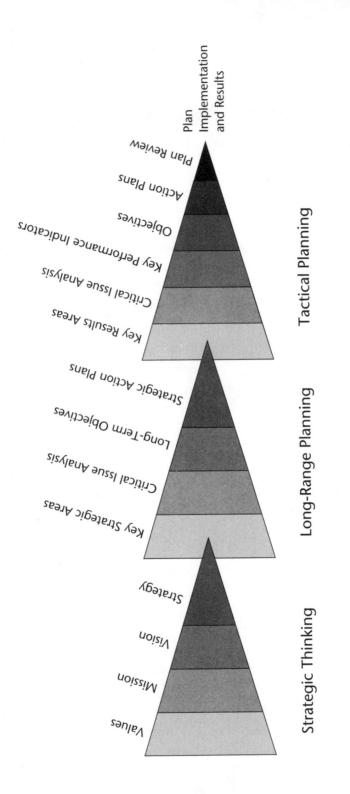

Figure 8.1 The Planning Process

Plan Implementation and Results

Plan Review
Action Plans
Objectives
Key Performance Indicators
Critical Issue Analysis
Key Results Areas

Tactical Planning

Strategic Action Plans
Long-Term Objectives
Critical Issue Analysis
Key Strategic Areas

Long-Range Planning

Strategy
Vision
Mission
Values

Strategic Thinking

You may choose to combine some of the elements or use them selectively, particularly if this is your first formal strategic planning effort or if your previous efforts did not produce the results you desired. Remember, never *adopt* any planning process, including this one. Always *adapt* it to what makes the most sense for your organization.

The Strategic Planning Assessment Checklist presented in Figure 8.2 is a tool that will help you both assess the readiness of your organization to proceed with a strategic planning effort and determine which elements need to be addressed to make your planning as effective as possible. (A similar checklist focused on tactical planning is included as Figure 9.1 in the third book of this series.) It provides a quick overview of what is involved in both strategic thinking and long-range planning, as well as an opportunity for pinpointing specific additions or modifications that may be required to make your approach as effective as possible.

When approaching this task from a total organization perspective, the initial assessment normally is made by the CEO, the senior management team, and/or the planning process facilitator. Individuals who may be given assignments related to one or more factors on the checklist need to understand and accept responsibility for whatever action may be expected. If you are examining this task from the perspective of your own unit, then you only need to focus on those factors that are relevant to your plan.

In making the assessment, you need to go through the checklist and place a check in the appropriate column for each item. *OK* means that your current strategic planning process addresses that item satisfactorily. It may need some fine tuning, but following existing practices is likely to produce the desired results. *Need* indicates that the item should be added or that a more effective application is required than the one you currently use. *N/A* should be checked if the item is either *not applicable* to your particular organization or unit or if it is incorporated elsewhere in your plan (combining *mission* and *vision*, for example). After completing the initial checks, review each of the items that has a check in the *Need* column and

Figure 8.2 Strategic Planning Assessment Checklist

	Current Status			Action (When and Whom)
	OK	Need	N/A	
Planning process established				
Plan to Plan				
Planning roles clarified				
• CEO/COO				
• Senior management team				
• Board				
• Planning facilitator				
• Planning coordinator				
• Internal planning staff				
• Other managers				
• Other employees				
Planning team selected				
Strategic Planning				
Strategic values				
Organization mission				
Unit missions				
Organization vision				
Organization strategy				
Key strategic areas				
Strengths/limitations				
Opportunities/threats				
Critical issues				
Analysis assignments				
Major conclusions				
Long-term objectives				
Financial projections				
Strategic action plan				
Executive overview				
Plan review/modification				
Strategic plan implementation				

Figure 8.3 Sample Completed Strategic Planning Assessment Checklist

	Current Status			Action (When and Whom)
	OK	Need	N/A	
Planning process established	✓			
Plan to Plan		✓		Draft by 1/5 — Martha
Planning roles clarified				
• CEO/COO	✓			
• Senior management team	✓			
• Board		✓		I will handle next meeting
• Planning facilitator		✓		Candidates identified 12/1 — Bill
• Planning coordinator	✓			
• Internal planning staff			✓	
• Other managers			✓	
• Other employees			✓	
Planning team selected	✓			
Strategic Planning				
Strategic values		✓		Handle first session
Organization mission	✓			May need some modification
Unit missions		✓		Recommendations 1/15 — Dept. Heads
Organization vision	✓			
Organization strategy		✓		Review & modify first session
Key strategic areas	✓			
Strengths/limitations		✓		Update first session
Opportunities/threats		✓		Update first session
Critical issues		✓		Update preplanning
Analysis assignments		✓		
Major conclusions		✓		
Long-term objectives		✓		
Financial projections		✓		
Strategic action plan		✓		
Executive overview		✓		
Plan review/modification		✓		
Strategic plan implementation		✓		

determine what action is required, by when, and by whom. The checklist highlights those portions of the strategic planning process that require special attention. It also provides a blueprint for getting started. Figure 8.3 provides an example of a checklist completed by a CEO.

How Do Unit Strategic Plans Fit In?

Unless your unit is the equivalent of a separate company—a division or subsidiary, for example, in which case you would apply the entire process as described in this book—you will probably use portions of the strategic planning process selectively. At the very least, in my judgment, every unit needs its own statement of roles and missions. Some departments, such as marketing and R&D, may find it desirable to go through the entire process, producing a miniversion of the total organization's plan as it relates to the department's responsibilities. Other departments, such as production and administration, may find it more useful to focus on specific strategic issues that directly impact their operations. Every unit in the organization, of course, needs to become familiar with those portions of the total organization's strategic plan, as well as with other units' plans, that will impact their own strategic and tactical efforts.

How Do We Pull It Together?

The creation of your strategic plan is no different from any other comprehensive effort. It requires the identification of what needs to take place and a realistic schedule for making sure that the planning process proceeds. An effective tool for doing this is a *Plan to Plan*. This is not just a play on words. A Plan to Plan clearly identifies significant steps in the strategic planning process that need to be completed if planning is to be an effective management tool. The Plan to Plan highlights the specific portions of the plan that need to be developed, sets a schedule for completion of each of these portions, and establishes a record of performance against that schedule.

Figure 8.4 is a sample Plan to Plan that includes a provision for unit plan development. Many variations are possible, of course, depending on the size of your organization and the amount of unit plan development required. You need to develop your own Plan to Plan, based on your specific planning requirements. Typically, the final event in the Plan to Plan will be review and approval by

---

Figure 8.4 Sample Strategic Plan to Plan

Objective: To complete the update of our strategic plan by May 15.

Action Steps	Timetable

1. Half-day preplanning meeting
  • Introduction to process
  • Advance assignments
	January 15

2. Two-day planning meeting
  • Strategic values
  • Organization mission
  • Organization vision
  • Organization strategy
  • Key strategic areas
  • Critical issues identification
  • Critical issue analysis assignments
	February 1–2

3. Undertake analysis assignments	February 3–28

4. Two-day planning meeting
  • Review of analysis assignments
  • Major conclusions
  • Long-term objectives
  • Financial projections
  • Strategic action plans
	March 1–2

5. Unit planning meetings (specific time varies)
  • Unit roles and missions
  • Critical issue analysis
  • Long-term objectives
  • Strategic action plans
	March 10–31

6. Integrate organization and unit plans	April 1–15
7. Document strategic plan	April 15–30
8. One-day planning meeting • Presentation, review, and approval of strategic plan	May 15

whoever has the final say. Usually there is a specific time frame within which approval must take place. Approval may be by a board of directors, a parent organization, a legislative body, or the CEO and the planning team themselves. By establishing a specific deadline by which approval must be obtained, it's possible to work backward and determine a realistic schedule for completion of each of the plan elements as well as submission of unit plans where appropriate.

What Does a Strategic Plan Look Like?

While each organization's strategic plan should be a direct reflection of the convictions and foresight of the CEO and the planning team, I have found it useful to separate the plan into three sections that are developed in reverse order.

The first section is an *executive overview*, which is a two- or three-page summary, usually in narrative form, that expresses the CEO's personal views on where the organization is headed, the principal philosophy and values overriding the way its business will be conducted in the future, and the major positions or accomplishments being projected for the life of the plan. This overview serves as the primary communication vehicle to those inside and outside the organization who have an interest in knowing what the future looks like for your organization.

The second section is a *condensed summary of the key elements* of your strategic plan. This includes your statements of mission, vision, and strategy (preferably on the same page), plus your key strategic areas, the long-term objectives related to each KSA, and where appropriate, major actions (not complete strategic action plans) required to reach your LTOs. This together with the executive overview is the primary strategic document distributed to your owners, parent organization, key employees, and other important stakeholders.

The third section contains *supporting materials* such as completed critical issue analyses, strategic action plans, selected department or unit strategic plans, and other related materials that will identify what needs to be done. Portions of this section will be made available as necessary to provide guidance for those who have to implement the plans.

Figure 8.5 shows a typical table of contents for a medium-size organization.

Figure 8.5 Sample Table of Contents for a Strategic Plan

	Page Number
1. Executive Overview	1–3
2. Summary of Key Plan Elements	4–10
• Organization mission, vision, strategy	4
• Key strategic areas, critical issues, long-term objectives, major actions, financial projections	5–10
3. Supporting Materials	11–25
• Each critical issue listed separately together with its completed analysis, long-term objectives, strategic action plans, and selected department plans	

When and How Do We Communicate Our Strategic Plans to Other Important Stakeholders?

Since your strategic plan is a major communication vehicle designed to keep other people with a need to know informed of what is happening within your organization, as well as to provide guidance to those who have to prepare and/or implement supporting strategic and tactical plans, you need to give careful consideration to when and how this communication should be handled. While there are some obvious stakeholders to whom your strategic plans are especially important, such as owners, shareholders, parent organization, peer and subsidiary organizations, and key employees, there may be others you wish to bring into your communication loop. These could include the financial and investment communities; your legal, accounting, and other outside advisers; strategic partners; major suppliers; major customers; outside sales representatives; friendly competitors; communities in which you are currently operating; communities where you may be operating in the future; professional and trade associations related to your industry; unions representing your employees; schools where you may be recruiting employees; the press; and perhaps the general public. Your decision to inform any or all of these groups of your strategic plans will depend on the value to both them and you of their being so informed. Once the various parts of your strategic plan are documented and approved, you will want to use them in any way that will prove mutually advantageous. (See Chapter Two for a discussion of ways of involving other stakeholders while your planning is in process.)

Aside from those who must approve your plans, your employees probably represent the single most important group to bring into the loop. Without their support, it will be difficult if not impossible for you to carry out your plans. It's important to get the word to them as quickly as possible, particularly if there are any potential surprises. You are far better off having them hear the news from you than through the grapevine or, worse still, the press. Handled properly, this communication can be a powerful way to bring your employees together in a united front. Here are some suggested ways to do this:

- Distribute copies of the executive overview and, possibly, the condensed plan; invite verbal, written, or electronic comments or suggestions.
- Use closed-circuit television, video, CD-ROM, E-mail, voice-mail, or other electronic media; invite comments or suggestions.
- Use your organizational newsletter, magazine, or other publications.
- Make a presentation at a general meeting of all employees, with opportunity for questions.

- Make presentations at small informal meetings by department, unit, or location, with opportunity for discussion with the CEO and/or other executives

Depending on the degree of involvement and commitment you want from some of your other stakeholder groups, your form of communication to them could range from an edited version of your executive overview to some of the same outlets suggested for use with employees.

While you may wish to keep some portions of your plan confidential for competitive reasons, your strategic plan normally is not something you should keep under lock and key, to which only the "anointed few" have access. It can be a powerful tool for building loyalty and getting commitment from all those who can help make your plans become reality.

In Summary

- A complete strategic plan includes the results of your strategic thinking and your long-range planning.
- Never *adopt* any planning process, including this one; always *adapt* it to what makes the most sense for your organization.
- The Strategic Planning Assessment Checklist is a tool that will help you assess your organization's readiness to proceed with a strategic planning effort and to determine which elements need to be addressed to make your planning as effective as possible.
- The strategic planning process may be applied selectively to individual units within your organization. Every unit needs to create its own statement of roles and missions; however, unit application could range from focusing on specific strategic issues affecting that unit to producing a miniversion of the total organization's plan as it relates to that unit's responsibilities.

- Every unit in the organization needs to become familiar with those portions of the total organization's strategic plan and with other units' plans that will impact their own strategic and tactical efforts.

- A Plan to Plan is an effective tool for identifying what needs to take place in your strategic planning effort and for establishing a realistic schedule for making sure that the planning process proceeds.

- A useful way to organize your strategic plan is to separate it into three sections:

  An *executive overview,* which is a two- or three-page summary, usually in narrative form, that expresses the CEO's personal views on where the organization is headed, the principal philosophy and values overriding the way its business will be conducted in the future, and the major positions or accomplishments being projected for the life of the plan

  A *condensed summary* of the key elements of your strategic plan, including your statements of mission, vision, and strategy, as well as your Key Strategic Areas, the long-term objectives related to each KSA, and where appropriate, major actions required to reach your LTOs

  Supporting materials such as completed critical analyses, strategic action plans, selected department or unit strategic plans, and other related materials that will identify what needs to be done

- Your strategic plan, or selected portions of it, are a major communications vehicle designed to keep other people with a need to know informed of what is happening within your organization, as well as to provide guidance to those who have to prepare and/or implement supporting strategic and tactical plans.

Your long-range plan is the middle component in the total planning process. It is designed to help you create the strategic journey necessary to carry out your organization's mission, vision, and strategy. Your long-range plan also provides a framework for preparing your short-term tactical plans, which will identify the specific results needed to keep you moving in the right direction.

Best wishes to you and your colleagues as you travel the road together to an exciting and fulfilling future!

Annotated Resources

I have found the following books useful in my study of management and planning practices. Most are recent publications, but I have also included a few classics that have influenced me greatly as I have proceeded on my own journey through the world of planning. This is not an exhaustive list. There are many other fine publications; these just happen to be ones that are meaningful to me. Since the subject matter of many of these titles overlaps the content in each of the three books in this series, the same set of annotated resources appears in each of them.

General Management and Management Tools

Applegate, Jane. *Strategies for Small Business Success*. New York: Plume/Penguin, 1995.

> This delightful book by a nationally syndicated columnist is both a compilation of some of her most popular columns and a collection of advice gathered from many small business entrepreneurs as well as from her own experience. The section on "Going Global" is especially worth reading by those who are anticipating moving into foreign markets.

Batten, Joe D. *Tough-Minded Leadership*. New York: Amacom, 1989.

> Joe Batten has been a close friend and colleague of mine for many years. As a writer and speaker, he has a unique talent for getting people to practice what they profess to believe. This book is a milestone piece of literature that provides clear direction for establishing a style of leadership that truly *expects* (and usually gets) performance that leads to outstanding results.

Bellman, Geoffrey M. *Getting Things Done When You Are Not in Charge: How to Succeed from a Support Position*. San Francisco: Berrett-Koehler, 1992.

Geoff Bellman addresses many of the frustrations that those of us who have been in support positions have experienced when trying to move our ideas through the corporate maze. We are not as powerless as we like to think we are. This book supports my concept of the *unit president*, showing practical ways of impacting organizational direction and results.

Block, Zenas, and MacMillan, Ian C. *Corporate Venturing: Create New Businesses in Your Firm*. Boston: Harvard Business School Press, 1993.
This book is designed for the internal champion, working under the corporate umbrella, who is charged with developing and marketing new ventures that are a distinct departure from the company's core products. Drawing on many real-world examples, it provides principles and techniques for making the new venture a success.

Collins, James C., and Porras, Jerry I. *Built to Last: Successful Habits of Visionary Companies*. New York: HarperCollins, 1994.
This book is a fascinating summary of research done with several companies the authors describe as *visionary* relative to several other successful but less-visionary companies in the same industries, all of which were founded before 1950. The "Twelve Shattered Myths" (such as "It takes a great idea to start a great company" and "Visionary companies require great and charismatic visionary leaders"), which are the theme of the book, provide eye-opening insights as well as methodologies for determining what makes the most sense for the future of your company.

Conner, Daryl R. *Management at the Speed of Change: How Resilient Managers Succeed and Prosper Where Others Fail*. New York: Villard Books, 1995.
Daryl Conner has been both a pioneer and a continual student in the field of change management. This book embodies the essence of his experience in working with a wide range of organizations as they move in dramatic new directions.

Drucker, Peter F. *Managing for the Future: The 1990s and Beyond*. New York: Truman Talley Books/Dutton, 1992.
Peter Drucker continues to be one of the world's most influential management thinkers, frequently years ahead of his time. This book presents a series of provocative and insightful essays under four broad headings: "Economics," "People," "Management," and "The Organization." "The Trend Toward Alliances for Progress" is a brief but precise set of guidelines for addressing one of the major business trends of the future.

Hammer, Michael, and Stanton, Steven E. *The Reengineering Revolution: A Handbook*. New York: HarperCollins, 1995.

This new book from the coauthor of *Reengineering the Corporation* addresses many of the successes and problems that have occurred within organizations that have undertaken reengineering efforts. It will be especially helpful to those managers who are seriously considering reengineering as a change methodology but who don't wish to get caught up in a "bandwagon" approach.

Leibfried, Kathleen H. J., and McNair, C. J. *Benchmarking: A Tool for Continuous Improvement.* New York: HarperCollins, 1992.
   This book from The Coopers & Lybrand Performance Solutions Series is the most comprehensive publication on the subject that I have seen. It emphasizes the importance of using this approach as *a never-ending objective* in maintaining the competitive edge.

Naisbitt, John. *Global Paradox: The Bigger the World Economy, the More Powerful Its Smallest Players.* New York: Morrow, 1994.
   John Naisbitt, of *Megatrends* fame, addresses the trend toward dramatic change in the ways that companies and countries do business. His premise is that "huge companies like IBM, Philips, and GM must break up to become confederations of small, autonomous, entrepreneurial companies if they are to survive." This is provocative reading from one of the foremost futurists of our time.

Osborne, David, and Gaebler, Ted. *Reinventing Government: How the Entrepreneurial Spirit Is Transforming the Public Sector.* Reading, Mass: Addison-Wesley, 1992.
   This is not a government-bashing treatise. It is a rational approach to using modern management principles and techniques to address the unique management concerns of government operations. The book is amply illustrated with examples of governmental entities that are doing this successfully at the national, state, and local levels.

Schmidt, Warren H., and Finnegan, Jerome P. *TQManager: A Practical Guide for Managing in a Total Quality Organization.* San Francisco: Jossey-Bass, 1993.
   Warren Schmidt and Jerry Finnegan have boiled down to the basics the concepts and competencies of the total-quality approach, without all the hoopla. If you want to learn how to make TQM work, this is the book to read.

Planning Theory and Practice

Allen, Louis A. *Making Managerial Planning More Effective.* New York: McGraw-Hill, 1982.

I had the privilege of working with Louis Allen in the mid 1960s while I was in a staff position at Rockwell International, to which he was serving as a consultant. He had a major impact on my managerial thinking and on my desire to become more involved in the planning process. This classic book provides comprehensive coverage of planning from the perspective of the individual manager rather than of the enterprise as a whole. Chapter Eight, "The Position Plan," is especially helpful for managers who need to define their own accountabilities as part of the total planning effort.

Austin, L. Allan, and Hall, Dean G. *COmpetitive REsourcing: How to Use Decision Packages to Make the Best Use of Human and Financial Assets*. New York: Amacom, 1989.

I have come to know Allan Austin as a brilliant strategic thinker with a strong international reputation. Few consultants in the field know how to address global competition as he does. This book is particularly directed toward managers in mature industries (those whose global market growth has dropped below 10 percent annually). Allan and his coauthor, Dean Hall, describe the COmpetitive REsourcing (CORE) process, which requires senior managers to identify their competitive gaps, establish strategies to reduce the gaps, and enlist the creativity and innovation needed from all levels of the organization to eliminate the gaps.

Below, Patrick J., Morrisey, George L., and Acomb, Betty L. *The Executive Guide to Strategic Planning*. San Francisco: Jossey-Bass, 1987.

This book helped establish the foundation from which the first two books in this series were derived. While I have made several modifications to the integrated planning process first introduced in *The Executive Guide*, the book still represents a sound approach to the strategic planning process.

Bryson, John M. *Strategic Planning for Public and Nonprofit Organizations: A Guide to Strengthening and Sustaining Organizational Achievement*. San Francisco: Jossey-Bass, 1988.

Recognizing that the principles and techniques of strategic planning are as important in the public and the nonprofit worlds as they are in corporate America, John Bryson shows how to make strategic planning work for city managers and administrators, cabinet secretaries, school superintendents and principals, sheriffs and police chiefs, elected and appointed officials of governments and public agencies, and boards of directors of nonprofit organizations.

de Bono, Edward. *de Bono's Thinking Course*, Rev. ed. United Kingdom: MICA Management Resources, 1994.

As de Bono says in the "Author's Note" in the book, "Thinking is the ultimate human resource. The quality of our future will depend entirely on the quality of our thinking. This applies on a personal level, a community level and on the world level." Since *strategic thinking* is a basic part of the planning process introduced in this series, I can think of no better source for learning the thinking process than one of the world's leading authorities on cognitive thinking.

Goodwin, B. Terence. *Write on the Wall: A How-To Guide for Effective Planning in Groups*. Alexandria, Va.: American Society for Training and Development (ASTD), 1994.

Since I am a strong proponent of the use of a skilled facilitator in the planning process, the title of this book caught my eye at a recent ASTD national conference. It is one of the most concise yet thorough guides to facilitation of the planning process that I have seen. I recommend it to anyone, brand new or experienced, who is charged with the responsibility of facilitating a group planning process.

Hamel, Gary, and Prahalad, C. K. *Competing for the Future: Breakthrough Strategies for Seizing Control of Your Industry and Creating the Markets of Tomorrow*. Boston: Harvard Business School Press, 1994.

One of the most insightful and provocative books to come out in recent years on preparing to make a difference in the marketplace of the future, this book is a wake-up call for managers who still believe that what has worked in the past will continue to produce the desired results in the future. One of the profound changes the authors see as necessary for those companies that expect to be successful in the future is the need to focus more on the development and enhancement of core competencies and less on gaining immediate market share. This is *must* reading for anyone who expects to compete successfully in the future.

Mintzberg, Henry. *The Rise and Fall of Strategic Planning*, New York: Free Press, 1994.

Although this appears to be an overt attack on strategic planning, it is more of a plea to do what is necessary to move an organization forward in meeting the challenges of the future. Mintzberg pulls no punches in assessing many of the accepted strategic planning theories and practices (if nothing else, it is entertaining reading in that respect). The final section of the book, "Planning, Plans, Planners," moves from the critical to the constructive, describing, among other factors, the new roles of planners as finders of strategy, as analysts, and as catalysts. His emphasis on coupling analysis and intuition helped clarify my thinking in drawing the distinctions among strategic thinking, long-range planning, and tactical planning.

Morrisey, George L. *Creating Your Future: Personal Strategic Planning for Professionals*. San Francisco: Berrett-Koehler, 1992.

>This book shows how to apply the principles and techniques of strategic planning to your own career growth, personal life, business development, and financial planning.

Morrisey, George L. *Management by Objectives and Results in the Public Sector* and *Management by Objectives and Results for Business and Industry*. Reading, Mass.: Addison-Wesley, 1976, 1977.

>These two books provide a how-to approach to making the MOR process work for managers in government and in business, respectively.

Morrisey, George L., Below, Patrick J., and Acomb, Betty L. *The Executive Guide to Operational Planning*. San Francisco: Jossey-Bass, 1987.

>This book, together with my prior books on Management by Objectives and Results, provided a foundation for the third book in this series, *A Guide to Tactical Planning*.

Odiorne, George S. *Management by Objectives: A System of Managerial Leadership*. New York: Pitman, 1965.

>George Odiorne was my colleague, mentor, and friend until his untimely passing a few years ago. This book was the one that put MBO on the map and helped make that concept one of the most enduring management "labels" of all time.

Odiorne, George S. *Strategic Management of Human Resources: A Portfolio Approach*. San Francisco: Jossey-Bass, 1984.

>This book is especially helpful for those who are required to analyze human resources in the strategic planning process. George shows how to apply portfolio analysis to human resource management and offers practical approaches for managing and capitalizing on high-performing employees.

Porter, Michael E. *Competitive Strategy: Techniques for Analyzing Industries and Competitors* and *Competitive Advantage: Creating and Sustaining Superior Performance*. New York: Free Press, 1980, 1985.

>These two landmark books provide a wealth of information on approaches and techniques for competitive analysis. They are especially useful for market analysts who are required to come up with the data needed to complete market segment analyses in highly competitive industries.

Ramsey, Jackson E., and Ramsey, Inez L. *Budgeting Basics: How to Survive the Budgeting Crisis*. New York: Franklin Watts, 1985.

>In searching libraries, I found very few books that addressed budgeting in anything other than "accountingese." This one is clearly the exception. It takes a potentially dry subject and puts it into clear, easy-to-read, nonfinan-

cial terms. The authors use a continuing case study throughout that is fun to follow. The chapter "New Department Budgeting" is especially helpful; it provides a good start-to-finish method, including how to make estimates on workload, human resource skills, materials, and operating costs. The book provides everything a nonfinancial manager needs to know, and then some, about what goes into the preparation of budgets.

Redding, John C., and Catalanello, Ralph F. *Strategic Readiness: The Making of the Learning Organization*. San Francisco: Jossey-Bass, 1994.

This book expands on the concept of the learning organization introduced in Peter Senge's *The Fifth Discipline* (New York: Doubleday, 1990). Its main focus is not on individual learning or team learning but on the organization-wide process through which entire firms plan, implement, and modify strategic directions. It moves beyond abstract descriptions of learning organizations and offers numerous illustrations of learning organizations in action.

Ruskin, Arnold M., and Estes, W. Eugene. *What Every Engineer Should Know About Project Management* (2nd ed.). New York: Marcel Dekker, 1995.

Project management is a very precise form of tactical planning, one that is bread and butter for most engineers. Arnie Ruskin has been a friend and colleague for many years. He and coauthor Eugene Estes have written one of the most practical books I have seen on the subject. The chapters on "Control Techniques" and "Risk Management" are especially useful for engineers and managers whose very survival may depend on assessing and controlling costs.

Steiner, George A. *Strategic Planning: What Every Manager Must Know*. New York: Free Press, 1979.

George Steiner's contributions to strategic and long-range planning are legendary. This book provides a comprehensive approach to strategic planning, including a wide variety of analytical techniques. It is especially useful for those wanting an in-depth understanding of the strategic planning process.

Tomasko, Robert M. *Rethinking the Corporation: The Architecture of Change*. New York: Amacom, 1993.

This is a refreshing look at the process of moving an organization from where it is now to where it needs to be, using the logic of the architect. Tomasko's sense of direction for the new corporation is: "It will be a business with few walls. Its structure will minimize barriers between staff thinkers and line doers, between functions and divisions, and between the company and the outside world."

Treacy, Michael, and Wiersema, Fred. *The Discipline of Market Leaders: Choose Your Customers, Narrow Your Focus, Dominate Your Market*. Reading, Mass.: Addison-Wesley, 1995.

The word *focus* is one of the most important words in the planning lexicon. This book brings this message home with a vengeance. The authors have identified three distinct value disciplines: *operational excellence, product leadership,* and *customer intimacy.* Their position, backed by real-world examples, is that companies that are real market leaders select one of these disciplines on which to stake their market reputation, even though they may continue to address the remaining two disciplines. Understanding these three value disciplines and how they work can be a significant step in the formulation of corporate strategy.

Tregoe, Benjamin B., and Zimmerman, John W. *Top Management Strategy: What It Is and How to Make It Work.* New York: Simon & Schuster, 1980; and Tregoe, Benjamin B., Zimmerman, John W., Smith, Ronald A., and Tobia, Peter M. *Vision in Action: Putting a Winning Strategy to Work.* New York: Simon & Schuster, 1989.

The first of these two books introduced the concept of the *driving force* as a powerful tool for determining strategy or strategic direction. It significantly influenced my and my coauthors' interpretation of strategy in our book *The Executive Guide to Strategic Planning.* The second book describes how the Kepner-Tregoe team has expanded and applied their approach to strategy in several well-known organizations, including addressing the perceptions of several managers within those organizations.

Weiss, Alan. *Making It Work: Turning Strategy Into Action Throughout Your Organization.* New York: HarperCollins, 1990.

The focus in this book is on implementation. Alan's premise is that the failure of strategies is most often not the result of poorly conceived strategies but rather the result of poor implementation. In an entertaining manner, he suggests some solid techniques for translating strategic thinking and long-range planning into real-world action.

Index